Tobiishi to International Karate League

Biography of Walter Nishioka Shihan

Cliff Field, M.D.

CJ Press

Published in 2011 by CJ Press

ISBN 978-0-9834554-1-7

Dedicated to

Pat Nishioka

Wife of Walter Nishioka whose sacrifices and support of Nishioka Shihan have helped shaped the International Karate League.

Foreword by Julian Shiroma

It is with great honor and privilege that I write this Foreword for Nishioka Shihan's biography.

Nishioka Shihan is the consummate martial artist. He pursued his interest in the martial arts with passion and fervor. He traveled abroad to train with the best and to learn from the best. He has taught thousands of students and produced numerous instructors, all the while leading by example.

His dedication, perseverance, humble demeanor, spirit of Aloha and strong sense of Ohana are unlike any teacher I have met. He inspires me to continue the journey to self perfection. He is truly Saiko Shihan, the Highest Master.

I credit Nishioka Shihan and his instructors for teaching and guiding me along my own rocky "tobiishi". Their combined efforts and wisdom helped me numerous times in facing life's challenges personally and professionally. No man or group of individuals have influence me greater than Nishioka Shihan and his cadre of instructors. I am forever grateful and indebted to them.

For those whole are contemplating learning a martial art, understand that all martial arts are good. It's the instructor that makes the difference. Nishioka Shihan, you will learn is such a person, a remarkable man.

In closing, I would like to thank and acknowledge Author Cliff Field, Sensei, for documenting the martial art life, travels, and experiences of Nishioka Shihan for the benefit of his students and all members of the martial art community.

With utmost respect, sincerity, and Aloha,

Julian H. Shiroma, Hanshi
Hachidan – International Karate League, Hawaii
Member – IKL Board of Governors

Foreword by Craig Hamakawa

Selflessness. This is the word I think about when describing Shihan, a very noble, giving person. I have had the good fortune of being in his presence & guidance since 1967. Shihan is an extremely generous person. His time, energy, knowledge, devotion knows no bounds. He has always tried to make his students become better people, not just better karateka's, better people. This does not happen by just training in karate, it becomes a way of life.

I can reflect back on my first encounter of Sensei Walter Nishioka in Hilo. My Sensei advised that you do not move unless Sensei Nishioka tells you to. Eventually my thighs cramped causing me to fall. Sensei Nishioka came over to massage (lomi lomi) my quadricep. Naturally, he inquired why I didn't stand up from the naihanchi stance. I was told not to, I responded. His response – how silly! At an early age, although fearing him to be god-like, I saw his sense of humor. It might have been compassion, but I was too afraid to ask.

I have many fond memories when I think of Shihan.

Tenacity – like practicing for a demonstration at the Blaisdell Arena, going through the attack moves over and over and over….each time absorbing blows to the midsection, only to be told – ONE MORE TIME!

Perseverance – to train like there is no tomorrow. To give your sweat, blood & tears to Honbu only to be told GAMBATTE!

Respectfulness – I have seen how other instructors in Honolulu have treated Shihan with the ultimate of respect. And yet, I have seen Shihan crouch to talk the shortest and youngest of students in the dojo. To learn to speak to everyone and anyone in the same manner is truly a gift.

Ability to teach an art form – training in karate takes dedication, commitment and a strong sense of self in learning this self-defense form. Shihan can teach the beginners as well as his senior students with ease. I have always marveled how he can communicate his thoughts in a manner that is easily digested by the masses.

Sense of humor – Shihan and I share a common bound. We are both born in the year of the Monkey. Suffice to say that Shihan is very Kolohe (Hawaiian), Warui (Japanese), Rascal type of person. He can be having a dead serious conversation and yet slip in a comment that if you weren't paying attention, you would miss his subtle approach at humor. I think he enjoys getting a good laugh with us. Or, at least I think he was laughing with us, not at us!

Good old fashion common sense – why would I want to teach you how to break bricks with your head. That's were your brains are residing. They better be there, son or you are in big trouble. Do you think I would ask that question again?

Father figure – I have always stated that I have had the good fortune of having 2 fathers. My father nurtured me. Shihan also nurtured me but in a different way. Each has had their unique way of developing me over time. Each has played a major role in shaping me as a person. Shihan is definitely the role model, the father figure of IKL for all of his students.

Enjoy the following passages that Dr. Clifford Field has provided you. You are journeying into the life & times of Shihan, Walter K. Nishioka. May we all be blessed with his character traits.

Craig H. Hamakawa, Hanshi
Hachidan – International Karate League, Mainland
Member – IKL Board of Governors

Contents

Preface

My own personal journey on writing this book began in 1997 with our first visit to Hawaii and training at Honbu. Nishioka Shihan, in his typical humble hospitality, insisted we have lunch with him. As my wife, Susan, and I listened to the stories he told that day the seed was planted for a desire to document the path he followed in martial arts, and equally important, the paths he did not take. Other Yudansha, Jeff Hara and Mel Teshima, had already written a brief historical account but as I listened to Shihan's stories I realized there was much more to add. Initially, this idea began with a simple short story that appeared in the IKL Newsletter. This story recounted when Shihan received a piece of jewelry made from black coral as a gift for teaching Karate in the Maui Dojo and this gift led to starting a jewelry business and providing many jobs on Maui.

As more visits to Hawaii led to hearing more stories, it became clear that there was much more to tell than what could be done in a few short stories. One particular story that started this project in earnest was how years ago on two occasions, previous attempts by others to compose a biography ended abruptly. The first attempt was prevented when flood waters in Roswell, New Mexico destroyed notes and memoirs that were being collected for research by a journalist. The second attempt at a biography was by a Honolulu journalist who, after a number of interviews with Shihan, met an untimely death with a heart attack. Shihan did not solicit these individuals to write about him. They knew his life and experience in the martial arts was already a story worth telling.

I asked Shihan if he would allow me to expand the short biographies already penned by yudansha's Jeff Hara and Mel Teshima. His response was, "Who would be interested in hearing my story?" I knew many would want to hear his story, just as my wife and I, so I began to put the stories into historical perspective and shared these with Shihan, repeatedly encouraging him to allow me to put the contents into a book. With much persuasion he finally agreed our students may be interested in how IKL came to be.

During the course of this project we found that Shihan felt the katas were more important to him than his own personal story. This resulted in a secondary project that produced the book "The Heart of the International Karate League" that discusses kata and the specific katas of IKL. The Heart of the International Karate League has an abbreviated biography of Nishioka Shihan. At first the book you are holding was to be the biography chapter of the kata book. However, Shihan felt the emphasis should be on kata and not him. He asked if we could condense the biography chapter in the kata book. This was done with the idea that a second book, this one, would detail his life in martial arts more thoroughly.

I choose the title "Tobiishi to International Karate League" because as the book came together it was apparent many choices and opportunities presented themselves to Nishioka Shihan throughout his life. Tobiishi are stepping stones found in a Japanese garden that lead one through the garden with a specific goal planned into the landscape. The opportunities presented to Shihan may have led him onto a different stepping stone (tobiishi) that followed a different path. If he had decided to follow one of these other paths I am confident he would have been just as successful. Fortunately for us, and the martial arts world, he followed the path of karate.

As he walked this path he and his wife, Pat, made many sacrifices to follow his passion. He devoted much of his lifetime to the pursuit of learning, understanding and teaching karate. Over his life, by following the Do of Karate, he has had a significant influence on others; martial arts colleagues, past and present students of IKL as well as non martial arts individuals. Nishioka Shihan continues to actively pursue this path. He continues to teach and attend seminars. He travels to all the IKL tournaments and events and he continues to create new katas. To see and experience the exuberance he continues to have for karate is inspiring; to appreciate his knowledge and experience is humbling.

I have come to appreciate Nishioka Shihan as one of the few remaining true masters of karate. His lifetime of dedication and pursuit of knowledge would be almost impossible to duplicate in this day. His desire and passion for learning and teaching is rare to find in an individual of any era. Nishioka Shihan has never desired monetary reward for his efforts and accomplishments. Instead his rewards go much deeper and are less tangible. However, they bestow a wealth that cannot be found by any other way. With all of his accomplishments he could rightfully be boastful, but instead he is the epitome of humbleness. All of these aforementioned traits are just the foundation for a true Master of his art. A foundation upon which a life's philosophy, a Do, is built upon. A philosophy that is succinctly stated in the IKL motto: Through Honesty and Sincerity comes Faithfulness, Respect, Effort and Etiquette.

I have been very fortunate to have had this opportunity to work on Shihan's biography. I have learned many things about a great man, a Master of Karate and the art of Karate. I cannot express enough gratitude to Nishioka Shihan and his wife, Pat Nishioka for allowing me to learn so much. I hope you enjoy reading this book as much as I did writing it.

Mahalo Nui Loa

Cliff Field
Yodan - IKL
IKL Membership Administrator
Ka'u Hospital Emergency Medical Director, Hawaii

Acknowledgements

Thanks to my wife, Susan, IKL Sandan, who helped take notes during the interviews with Shihan and also helped proof read this book.

Thanks to Jeff Hara, IKL Rokudan and IKL Board Member and Mel Teshima, IKL Shichidan and IKL Board Member, for providing material that provided many starting points for the interviews.

Thanks to Robert Matsushita, IKL Sandan, for digitizing many of the photos for IKL's 50th Anniversary event that were also used in this book.

Walter Kenmotsu Nishioka Shihan

Introduction

On reflection of one's life it is interesting to see how we arrived where we are today. Life is like following a path through the woods or a garden. The path leads to a goal but along the way we may experience the unexpected or come to a fork in the path. In the woods the trail may be marked or in a Japanese Garden there may be stepping stones (to-biishi) to help guide our way. Or we may decide to step off

1

the beaten path and take an entirely new approach, leaving a trail for others to follow. What is more important than the goal is the adventure and experience we live in reaching it.

Reflecting back on the life of Walter Kenmotsu Nishioka Shihan, we see the path he took that resulted in the creation of a new style of karate. This new style went on to become the International Karate League.

The Early Years

The year is 1932. Unemployment in the United States reached 33% and tensions were developing throughout the world as Japan continued to occupy more of China and events in Germany would eventually lead to World War II. Hawaii will not be a State for another 27 years. It is on June 18th in the Kalihi District of Honolulu when our story begins.

On June 18th, 1932, Kiyo Nishioka gave birth to Walter Kenmotsu[1] Nishioka. His father, Hikoki Nishioka, and his mother, both from the Kumamoto Prefecture[2] in Japan immigrated to Hawaii in 1907. Walter Nishioka was in a family with three brothers and four sisters.

At a very early age, Walter Nishioka began learning Jujitsu[3] from his father. His father taught the Japanese Imperial

---

1   Kenmotsu can be translated as "holder of the sword".

2   Kumamoto Prefecture is located on Japan's southernmost island Kyushu. Prefectures are sub national jurisdictions created in 1871 when the feudal Han system was abolished.

3   Jujitsu, or the art of suppleness, probably emerge as a martial art in the 1600's but it is unclear who was responsible or where this occurred. The main focus of jujitsu is its effectiveness in combat where encounters were often lethal.

Marines[4] in Kyushu while he still lived in Japan. Walter Nishioka began learning jujitsu because he wanted to learn how to defend himself. He was small for his age and lived in a rough district of Honolulu and he did not want to get "beat up" by the other boys.

Seishiro Okazaki

Hikoki Nishioka continued teaching his son jujitsu until 1940 at which time Walter Nishioka began Jujitsu studies with Seishiro Okazaki. Professor Okazaki was the founder of the American Jujitsu Institute in Hawaii and the founder

---

4   Prior to 1920 the Japanese Navy had special landing forces called rikusentai which were the ship's individual crew members that received infantry training. These landing forces went on to be known as the Imperial Marines.

of Danzan-ryu.[5] Helping Okazaki were many of his senior students including Takamoto, Hamamato, Guzman and Jack Wheat. Hamamoto also taught Karate, Kendo, stick fighting techniques and yawara, a martial art of breaking holds. Because of his previous training with his father Walter Nishioka was promoted to green belt within the first week by Takamoto Sensei. At age 16 he received his Shodan in Jujitsu from Professor Okazaki.[6] He continued to train in Jujitsu under Sensei Okazaki and Okazaki's disciples until he was 18 years old.

On December 7th 1941, Walter Nishioka was at home playing outside when many planes began to fly over head. Soon

---

5   Danzan-ryu is interpreted as "Hawaiian Style". Professor Seishiro Okazaki (1890 - 1951) originally lived in Hilo, HI after moving from Japan. In 1929 he moved to Honolulu where he opened the Okazaki Adjustment and Restoration Sanitorium, later named the Nikko Restoration Sanitorium. Okazaki practiced Seifukujutsu, a form of deep massage and balancing of energy flow (Ki) in the body where the therapist uses their elbow. The sanitorium was also used as a place to teach Jujitsu.

6   There is an interesting side history concerning Jujitsu and Judo. During this era, Japan and its Emperor were doing away with the Samurai class and trying to appear more civilized to the rest of the world. Jujitsu was a martial art that was considered "non-gentle", i.e. it was meant to harm. As a result of this cultural transition in Japan, Judo (gentle way) was created by Jigoro Kano. Jigoro Kano was a student of Jujitsu and in 1882 formulated a new system based on Jujitsu but added many guiding principles and rules which made Judo a "sport" martial art compared to jujitsu. He went on to develop the respected Kodokan Judo School. Jigoro Kano received Japan's First Order of Merit from the Emperor of Japan for founding Judo.

he could hear the explosions of bombs being dropped at Pearl Harbor. Nishioka Shihan recalls it was a frightening moment, with one bomb exploding within a couple miles of his parent's home.

After the bombing of Pearl Harbor, Japanese Americans were forcibly placed in internment camps throughout the country. In 1942 there were more than 150,000 Japanese Americans living in the Hawaiian Territory, composing more than a third of its population. Even under these circumstances almost 1800 were placed in camps throughout the islands. Hikoki Nishioka was taken by the Military Police to one of these camps because of his past association with the Japanese Imperial Marines when he lived in Japan.

Honouliuli Internment Camp where Shihan's father was interned during the war. This camp was at present day Ewa Beach area on Oahu.

At that same time, two of Walter Nishioka's older brothers were in the United States Military[7] service during WW II; one eventually was stationed in occupied Japan. One brother talked to his commanding officer about his father being held in an internment camp. This eventually led to Hikoki Nishioka's release after 1 1/2 years being held prisoner. Nishioka Shihan recalls the day the MPs returned his father. At first he was fearful they were there to take his mother away, but then he saw his father exiting the car to return home.

---

7   Cards were placed in the windows of homes indicating how many sons were serving in the Military. The Nishiokas had two cards for their sons in WWII. They could have placed a third card when Nishioka Shihan joined the service but did not want to be boastful, so continued to display only two cards. Nishioka Shihan could also have received a deferral because he had two brothers in the service but instead elected to enlist when he was old enough.

The Military Tobiishi

Just as the 20th century reached its midpoint, a few years after the end of World War II, the United States was in a unique position in the world. There was no postwar recession as seen between WW I and WW II. While Europe and Japan were rebuilding from the war's destruction, the United States industries assumed a leading role in the world economy. The United States dollar became the world's major reserve currency.

During the Allied occupation of Japan (until 1952) and with the help of United States financial aid, Japan saw the restoration of a Democratic Party government, women gained the legal right to vote and a true parliamentarian state was developed. Japan regained its independence with the signing of the peace treaty in 1951.

Around the same time, just across the Sea of Japan, hostilities were beginning between North and South Korea. These hostilities were an attempt by both Koreas to reunify the country under their respective governments. With both sides supported by external powers, this conflict eventually became known as the Korean War.

In 1950 Walter Nishioka graduated from McKinley High School in Honolulu, Hawaii. In his senior year he joined the

Naval Reserves at the age of 17. While in the Naval Reserves he would go to Pearl Harbor once a week to study. He recalls being on a submarine just off Diamond Head's shore when it caught fire. Although he was in the naval reserves Walter Nishioka always had a desire to fly so shortly after graduation, he volunteered for active duty in the United States Air Force. In doing so, he received an honorable discharge from the Naval Reserves at age 19.

Walter Nishioka's Air Force basic training was at Lackland Air Force Base in San Antonio, Texas. Many skills were taught and tested during basic training. These tests helped the military decide what assignment was best suited for the soldier. One skill Walter Nishioka excelled at was sharp shooting. Even though he never shot a gun before, he placed second during a sharp shooting assessment, just missing first place by a few points. This superior marksmanship is valued in an aerial gunner so he was assigned to gunnery school at Lowry Air Force Base in Denver, Colorado. Here he learned to be an aerial gunner on the B-29 bomber and the B-26 dive bombers.

Walter Nishioka and the B-29 Superfortress

After completing gunnery school he was transferred to Walker Air Force Base in the Strategic Air Command (SAC) at Roswell, New Mexico. He was assigned to a flight crew attached to the 509th bomber squadron and was awaiting deployment to active duty in the skies over Korea.[8] This is when destiny stepped in and presented an opportunity to Walter Nishioka; a fork in the garden's path. The fateful stepping stone (tobiishi) Shihan took was to attend a judo exhibition at Walker Air Force Base. The exhibition was conducted by Master Sergeant John Hodges[9] who was stationed at Walker Air Force Base. Walter Nishioka's fellow airmen knew of his training in jujitsu and judo and told him of the exhibition. When they attended the exhibition, his fellow airmen told Master Sergeant Hodges there was a judo man named Walt Nishioka in the audience. During the demonstration Master Sergeant Hodges asked if Airman Nishioka was in the audience and if he would come help in the demonstration. The humbleness and respect Nishioka Shihan had, even at this young age, prevented him from doing this, but after the demonstration he introduced himself to Master Sergeant Hodges.

---

8   The Korean War was the last major war where propeller powered fighters were used. This is the first war where the Soviet-made MiG-15 jet fighters were used by North Korea and the F-86 Sabre by the United States. Over the course of the war at least 16 B-29 bombers were shot down by communist aircraft.

9   Sergeant John Hodges instructed FBI agents prior to World War II and worked with the resistance guerrillas in the Philippines during World War II.

Walter Nishioka with his "boss", Master Sergeant
John Hodges at Walker AFB, Roswell, New
Mexico

Master Sergeant Hodges knew the value of an airman well
trained in judo and jujitsu who could help teach his training programs. Master Sergeant Hodges had Shihan's orders
changed so he could help Hodges train other airmen. Instead
of deployment to active duty in Korea, Corporal Walter Nishioka was assigned to the Flight Survival Training Program
at Walker Air Force Base and assisted with instructing flight

Walker AFB Judo team 1953. Walter Nishioka standing. His "boss", Sgt. Hodge is on his right.

Walker AFB Judo Team - 1955

Left to Right; Assistant instructor John Baca (heavy-weight), Assistant instructor Alan Dow (150 lbs div), Head instructor Walter Nishioka (130 lbs div), Assistant instructor Carl Royal (180 lbs div)

Walter Nishioka with "buddies" at Lackland Air Force Base - 1951

Left: General Mus-
grave's son throwing
Walter Nishioka during
Judo demonstration at
the base's officers club.

Judo demonstration at an Officer's Club at Walker AFB 1953. Walter Nishioka is the person executing the throw on Sgt. William Wick.

crews in the Survival Training Course and Flight Crew Combat courses. These courses taught basic hand-to-hand combat techniques to flight crews who may have had to bail out behind enemy lines and work their way back to allied lines.

The Survival Training Flight Crew Combat Course was the idea of General Curtis LeMay. General LeMay, a four star General, was the commanding general of SAC and in 1951. He wanted a training program created for SAC flight crews. Emile Bruno[10] was appointed to oversee the program. Many of the judo instructors at the bases were civilians so recruiting experienced airmen was a priority for the program. While these courses were being taught in the United States by experienced instructors, Judoka Emile Bruno was initiating training for additional instructors in Japan by sending groups of airmen to the Kodokan Institute for training.

The offer of being an instructor presented a difficult decision for Walter Nishioka. He always wanted to fly and serve his country; he wanted to go on at least one mission. Members of his gunnery training team encouraged him to go be an instructor with the survival training program, pointing out he could help more flight crews in that position. With much deliberation, Walter Nishioka choose the path of the Survival Traiising instructor. Today he sadly recollects some of the members in his class at the gunnery school were shot down or had to bail out behind enemy lines and were never heard of again.

---

10   Emile Bruno had his 5th Dan in Judo and was a former National AAU Wrestling Champion. Bruno was a civilian instructor. General Lemay was a judo student and trained under Bruno.

In the Survival Training Course, Master Sergeant Hodges had two assistants helping with the courses: Corporal Walter Nishioka and Sergeant Ed "Brook" Maley.[11] Sergeant Maley, who was already a Judoka as a civilian, was described by Nishioka Shihan as a "tough big guy who diligently worked out and was a very well versed instructor".

SAC Judo Tournament 1953.
Lt. to rt: General Musgrave, Walter Nishioka, Edwin Maley. Walter Nishioka coached and trained with Sgt. Maley who was the 180 lb. Champion

Sergeant Maley and Corporal Nishioka would share responsibilities in assisting Master Sergeant Hodges in teaching and also do the physical conditioning for the flight crews. When flight crews would return from long flights they immedi-

---

11   Sergeant Ed Maley was from Brooklyn, hence the nickname "Brook". Professor Ed Maley currently operates the Florida School of Judo. He has his Hachidan in Judo (8th degree) from Kodokan Judo Institute World Headquarters in Tokyo, Japan.

ately reported for physical conditioning. Physical conditioning consisted of calisthenics, followed by a steam room and massage before returning to their squadron. This was to prevent fatigue and injuries in the flight crews.

Master Sergeant Hodges and Sergeant Ed Maley were transferred to Carswell SAC Base outside of Fort Worth, Texas, to begin a similar training program. As a result Walter Nishioka became the head instructor of the survival course at Walker Air Force Base. He had to train two airmen to become his assistant instructors to help teach the course and conduct the physical conditioning.

Walter Nishioka would teach up to three bomber crews at a time, with each crew having eight airmen. Each crew had airmen of different ranks and approximately 16 higher ranking officers. He would tell the flight crew members that when in the Survival Training Course they were to leave their rank in the locker room; as their teacher he was the boss.

Rarely, he would have a new student try to challenge him; partly because they were physically much larger. However they quickly learned "dynamite comes in small packages" as they became the subjects of class demonstrations. Through these actions, the students became very respectful of him just as he was always respectful of his students. Many of the ranking officers would pass him on the base and say "Hi Walt" while exchanging salutes. This impressed his fellow airman that an officer would address him in such a familiar way. Walter Nishioka would simply reply that they were his students.

SAC tour instructors from Japan (circa 1953) visiting Mt. Rushmore while at Ellsworth AFB. Standing Lt. to rt: Ohtake Sensei (Roku-dan- Judo), Ishikawa Sensei (Rokudan-Judo), Kazuo Kobayashi (Godan - Judo), Sato Sensei (Judo and Tachiwaza), Kenji Tomiki (Hachidan - Aikido) and Hosokawa Sensei (Judo). Front row (Lt. to rt): Unknown host, Isao Obata (Yodan - Shoto-kan), Sumiyuki Kotani (Hachidan-Judo), Toshio Kamada (Sandan - Shotokan), Hidetaka Nishiyama (Sandan - Shotokan).

Eventually the training programs incorporated judo, aikido, and karate into the courses. This worked so well that General LeMay wanted this type of instruction expanded in the United States.

This resulted in the legendary 1953 SAC tour where ten Japanese martial artists where invited to a three month tour of the Air Force bases to teach their disciplines. Coordinating this tour from Japan were members of the Kodokan Judo Institute. They choose the instructors that would represent the selected martial arts.

Shotokan practitioners were chosen to represent Karate. They included some of Gichin Funakoshi's best students: Toshio Kamata, Isao Obata and Hidetaka Nishiyama. Hidetaka Nishiyama became one of the founders of the Japan Karate Association and upon moving to the United States in his later years founded the All American Karate Federation (AAKF). Aikido was represented by Kenji Tomiki who was a student of Aikido's founder Morihei Ueshiba as well as a student of Judo's founder, Jigoro Kano. Kenji Tomiki went on to be the founder of Tomiki Aikido (aka Shotokan Aikido) and the Japan Aikido Association. The Judoka were Kazuo Kobayashi, Sumiyuki Kotani, Kusuo Hosokawa, Ohtake Sensei, Sato Sensei and Ishikawa Sensei. Ohtake Sensei taught locks, restraints and strangle holds. Sato Sensei taught tachiwaza which is a judo technique used to unbalance an opponent. Hosokawa Sensei taught methods to disarm an opponent.

There were three SAC Air Forces involved in the tour; the 2nd, the 8th, and the 15th. Walter Nishioka Shihan was assigned to be a student and interpreter for the "Mighty 8th "[12].

Later in 1954, the Air Force wanted training videos created and distributed to be used as a reference for the hand to hand combat techniques. Paramount Studios was contracted for the filming. Corporal Walter Nishioka, Captain "Red" Purvis[13], three instructors from the 2nd, 8th and 15th Air Force, and three civilian judo teachers were chosen to make these films. These films were created in two parts. One was filmed indoors, at Paramount Studios, U.S. Army Signal Corp. Center in Long Island New York. This month-long filming covered the basics of various judo throws, knife techniques by Capt. "Red" Purvis and Tomiki pivot points. The second part was filmed outdoors in the swamp jungle areas outside of Tampa's McDill Air Force base. This filming also took a month and showed application of the techniques in choreographed skits to simulate a jungle combat situation including strangle locks and knife work.

In addition to the videos, General LeMay also wanted the instructors to have ongoing seminars. A year after the SAC tour Walter Nishioka attended a week long seminar at Offut Airforce Base in Nebraska. In attendance were General Lemay, and the Judoka, Ohtake Sensei and Hosokawa Sensei from the 1953 SAC tour.

---

12   The 8th Air Force is known as the Mighty 8th. While stationed at Walker AF base Nishioka Shihan participated in the SAC Judo tournaments. He became the coach and manager of the team which won the 8th AF team championship in 1953.

13   Captain Purvis was adept in the art of knife combat.

Walter Nishioka's military discharge came in September of 1955. The Air Force wanted him to reenlist and continue to teach. They offered him a noncom officer rank if he would stay. In addition, the Marines[14] tried to recruit him to become a drill Sergeant and offered him the rank of Sergeant. Instead, Shihan elected to take an honorable discharge as Airman First Class. Even though the military provided many opportunities, he wanted to return home to Hawaii.

Nishioka Family Mon or Family Seal. Most family seals are derived from patterns drawn from things like flowers and birds. These designs originated in the Asuka period (6c-8c) but most of the patterns that serve as the basis of today's family emblems were used in the Heian period (9c-12c). In the Muromachi period and the following Warrior Society (15c-16c), these family seals became heraldic markings used by the warrior class. They played a significant role in the warrior society of that time. This eventually became a symbol of one's family name and played a significant role as a symbol of lineage.

The Nishioka Mon is based on a kikkyo; a small purple flower.

---

14   A Marine recruiter who was a friend of Sergeant Hodges would often attend and watch the classes he and Shihan taught. When he learned of Shihan's upcoming discharge he tried to recruit Nishioka Shihan into the Marines.

Walter Nishioka and combat instructor Sgt. Carl Flood, at Paramount indoor studio in Long Island, New York

Nishioka Shihan in a simulated jungle attack on one of his flight crew students burying his parachute in enemy territory

Instructors in Paramount Training Film. Nishioka Shihan is in the second row, second from the right. Emil Bruno (far left, back row) was chosen by General Lemay to head the SAC Judo instructions.

The Japanese Tobiishi

The late 1950s were part of an era when the United States continued to show prosperity. With the Korean War over and Europe and Japan just beginning to restore their economy the United States solidified its industrial and financial leadership in the world. Despite the growing fear of communism from the Soviet Union, the Cold War and the public's ignorance that President Eisenhower had sent advisers to Vietnam, there was a general feeling of well-being and prosperity in the United States. The general outlook of the country was reflected in it's pop culture with the number one song "Rock Around the Clock" by Billy Haley and His Comets, the number one TV show was $64,000 question and McDonald's opened its first restaurant. Gasoline was only $.23 a gallon, a postage stamp was three cents and Disneyland first opened its gates.

As a civilian, Walter Nishioka returned to Hawaii and with him he brought a vast knowledge of martial arts with the experience and ability to teach it. Upon returning to Hawaii he began working at the Hawaii State psychiatric hospital. As the Charge Aide his duties were similar to that of a LPN (Licensed Practical Nurse). He would give injections to patients and specialized in administrating electroshock therapy.

It wasn't long until he began teaching martial arts to some of the psychiatrist and the hospital's CEO. The doctors would try to renew their contracts with the hospital just so they could stay and continue their martial arts instructions with Nishioka Shihan. Because of this relationship with the doctors and CEO, he was able to follow the next stepping stone on the martial art's path; travel to Japan and other Asian countries to learn more about martial arts. The hospital's CEO knew he would also benefit from this endeavour, so Shihan was able to take three months off each year while working at the hospital (1956–1960) to travel to Japan. The American dollar was very strong compared to the Japanese yen and he could save enough money in nine months to finance his trips to Japan. Three meals a day could be bought for a dollar and accommodations cost $35 a month in the inexpensive dormitories at Kodokan Judo Institute[15].

While in Japan the instructors Nishioka Shihan met during the Strategic Air Command tour invited him to come visit their schools. He attended Kodokan Judo Institute[16] with Professor Sumiyuki Kotani and Professor Kusuo Hosokawa, among others. He studied Aikido techniques with Tomiki Sensei and Shotokan (Nihon Karate Association) with Hidetaka Nishiyama Sensei in Yotsuya, Tokyo where Gichin Funakoshi had been the teacher many years earlier.

Many of these instructors requested that Nishioka Shihan stay with their school, knowing their style would get excel-

---

15   The Kodokan Judo Institute was founded in 1882 by Kano Jigoro. Kodokan means: Ko - to lecture; do- the way; kan - public hall. Physically it occupies an eight story building in Tokyo. The floors serve different purposes such as Judo research, Training and dormitories.

16   While attending the Kodokan Judo Institute Nishioka Shihan was awarded a Black Belt in Judo.

lent representation and exposure in the United States upon his return to Hawaii. Some offered him high ranking black belts[17] which he would humbly not accept. Nishioka Shihan was not concerned with Dan ranking; he just wanted to learn martial arts. If he did except such an offer, proper etiquette would require he stay with that school. Instead Nishioka Shihan knew that there was much more to learn about karate and martial arts than any one school could offer.

After the Korean War some servicemen from Hawaii remained in Japan and were residing at the Kodokan dormitories. Shihan knew these servicemen and they helped direct him to other schools beyond his exposure with the Strategic Air Command tour. He studied with various Senseis and Sempais from different styles such as Shotokan, Shito Ryu and Goju ryu. This is how he discovered Wado Ryu and its founder Ohtsuka Sensei.

Nishioka Shihan's introduction to Wado Ryu, also known at that time as the All Japan Karate League, was in 1959. His first exposure to Wado Ryu was through Professor Yoshio Kawaguchi. Through Kawaguchi, he was introduced to Hironori Ohtsuka and Ohtsuka's "right hand man": Professor Tatsuo Suzuki.

---

17   At this time many styles had switched to the ju-dan ranking system. Wado Ryu, continued to use a belt ranking on a Go-dan ranking system with Go-dan being the highest rank. Nidan would be equivalent to Shichidan in the Ju-dan ranking schema.

Professor Yoshio Kawaguchi is still considered by Shihan to be his Sensei. Kawaguchi was the head instructor of the Yokohama Branch of Wado Ryu when Shihan trained under him. Shihan also earned a Black belt from Kawaguchi around 1960. In 2008, despite being very ill, Kawaguchi came to Hawaii just to visit Shihan. He visited with his wife and a disciple by the name of Hiroshi Sato. Kawaguchi succumbed to his poor health in 2009.

Tatsuo Suzuki (1928 -) began training under Ohtsuka Sensei in 1945 and went on to be his senior student. He traveled with Ohtsuka for demonstrations and teaching. He eventually moved to England where he founded the Wado Federation of England and later established the Wado International Karate-Do Federation. In addition to karate he holds a 2nd Dan in Tenshin Koryu Bo-Jitsu (Stick fighting) and a 1st Dan in Judo. He also studied Zen doctrine with high priests.

Hironori Ohtsuka (1892 – 1982) began his studies as a youth in martial arts with Jujitsu just as Nishioka Shihan did. Ohtsuka trained under Gichin Funakoshi (founder of Shotokan) and Kenwa Mabuni (founder of Shito-Ryu) and studied Kobudo (weapons art). Ohtsuka eventually went on to merge Okinawan karate with Japanese jujitsu into what became Wado Ryu in 1934. Wado-ryu's (Way of Harmony) aim is the development of a mind that is tranquil but alive and not just physical conditioning. This mind could act intuitively without hesitation. Ohtsuka was a physician who left his practice to instruct full time. Hironori Ohtsuka was awarded the First Order of Merit from the Emperor of Japan for his dedication and creating Wado-ryu.

Ohtsuka's philosophy on Karate is that it is an art that is healthy for the mind and body and by practicing it, leads one to serenity and humbleness. With this humbleness you respect other's rights and accept people for who they are. The more you train, the stronger you become and the more humble you become. "Just like a bamboo culm that will bend but not break".

Ohtsuka saw Wado Ryu primarily as a spiritual discipline where "Ten-Chi-Jin, Ri-Do" (Heaven-Earth-Man, Principal-Way) was a union to be respected and sought through discipline and dedication. This philosophy inspired Shihan and, as a dedication to Ohtsuka, eventually resulted in Shihan creating the kata Tenchi. Ohtsuka visited Shihan in Hawaii in 1961 and saw a portrait of Shihan done by Fred Guzman. Shihan was in a forward stance while executing a soto uke and tetsui. Ohtsuka commented that it was "Tenchi" and it was a very good defense that would be hard to penetrate

Ohtsuka Sensei was a very busy man but despite that, he took five days to show Shihan some of his dojos outside of Tokyo. Nishioka Shihan describes Ohtsuka as a very humble man and told Nishioka Shihan if he wanted to learn Wado Ryu that Kawaguchi was the one to train with in Yokohama[18].

---

18   Yokohama is the capital of the Kanagawa Prefectures (similar to states in the US) and a major port of Japan. It is the second largest city and is located on the western coast of Tokyo Bay.

While staying at the Kodokan Judo Institute Nishioka
Shihan would train in Judo at night. During the day he
would travel to Yokohama to train with Yoshio Kawaguchi.
In his spare time he trained privately with Ohtsuka at Meiji
University. It was during these private instructions that Ohtsuka
would teach Nishioka Shihan katas outside the Wado-ryu
system.

Yoshio Kawaguchi in 2009

Wado-ryu training was unique because it was the only karate style that had kumite drills. Contrary to Ohtsuka's belief, Gichin Funakoshi did not believe tournaments were necessary and thus there was no kumite training. This belief was based on historical martial arts training where it was used for defense or for war and practicing deadly techniques on each other would only harm the student or warrior. Ohtsuka felt kumite training was important so he introduced yakusoku, and later jyu kumite into the Wado curriculum. Yakusoku, or two man waza (technique), was a prearranged series of attacks and defenses between two students. This made kumite drills safer for the students but allowed the benefits of kumite training. This eventually led to tournament or "sport" kumite (jyu) competition. This difference in philosophy was the reason Ohtsuka departed Funakoshi's School and started his own style.

Hironori Ohtsuka and Tatsuo Suzuki

Hidetaka Nishiyama

Tatsuo Suzuki

Yamaguchi Gogen

The training Nishioka Shihan did was very intense and lasted all day long, every day of the week. During his free time from Wado Ryu and Judo training he would attend and train in other styles to expand his experience and knowledge. He trained with Hidetaka Nishiyama[19] and became close friends with Hirokazu Kanazawa[20] in Shotokan. He also trained in Goju-ryu with Yamaguchi Gogen[21] and various Shito-ryu schools. The training was not only physically difficult; it was also difficult because outsiders were not openly welcomed. This was especially true for an American outsider. Many of the dojo's students were college age and they had their opinions of American tourists. They felt Americans were rich braggarts and appeared arrogant because they won the war against their country. Because of these feelings they trained more aggressively when paired with Nishioka Shihan, almost to the point of trying to "beat him up". However, in addition to being able to hold his own in class, Shihan always remained humble and grateful for the experience.

---

19   Hidetaka Nishiyama (1928-2008) was a student of Gichin Funakoshi (Shotokan). He helped establish the Japan Karate Association. In 1961 he moved to Los Angeles and founded the All American Karate Federation.

20   Hirokazu Kanazawa (1931 - present) was a student of Nishiyama. He went on to establish the Shotokan Karate-do International, U.S.A. Nishioka Shihan would exchange training and teaching ideas with each other.

21   Yamaguchi Gogen (1909-1989) was one of the most renowned karate master from Japan. A student of Chojun Miyagi, Gogen founded the International Karate Goju-kai Association.

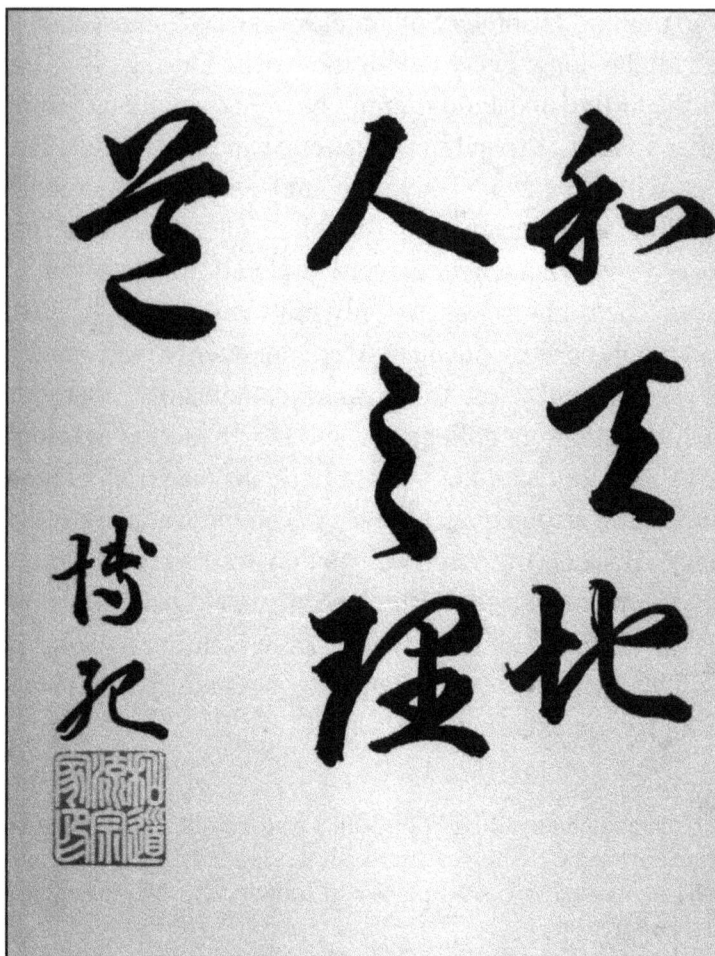

Brush calligraphy by Ohtsuka presented as a gift to Nishioka Shihan. It reads: "Tenchi jin ba wasuru wa kore rini kanau michi" - "When the sky and the earth and a person become one, it matches reason."

To show his gratitude Nishioka Shihan would often dine with many students after class at nearby restaurants and would insist on paying for the meals or request the waitress bring certain dishes. Nishioka Shihan did this out of generosity and wanted to show how he appreciated the opportunity to participate and learn in class. He wanted to give something back to the students for allowing him to participate in class.

The students were unaccustomed to this behavior from an American; especially from one they would try to punish in training. Impressed by his ability to withstand the difficult training and his desire to give back to their school the students soon accepted him as one of their own. This was unusual at the time considering the impressions the Japanese had of most Americans. Nishioka Shihan explained to his fellow students that it was the strength of the dollar that made Americans appear rich. Nishioka Shihan also explained that most tourist were not there to brag or be arrogant. They were there because they loved Japan and were interested in Japanese culture. They learned that Nishioka Shihan was not a wealthy man but just wanted to learn martial arts and made many sacrifices to travel to the countries where different styles originated. Through his actions and words he became an ambassador of good will. Nishioka Shihan still has strong feelings today that karate should show camaraderie, a family spirit and an attitude of generosity toward your fellow karateka based on a principle of helping your colleagues.

In 1960 Nishioka Shihan left his work at the hospital and entered a partnership in the slipper[22] business. In 1961 Shihan began teaching karate on Maui. The students wanted to show their appreciation so they gave him a gift. This gift was a piece of black corral jewelry which Nishioka Shihan humbly accepted. Upon return to his home in Oahu, Shihan showed the jewelry to his wife, Pat. She immediately appreciated its beauty.

Mrs. Nishioka told her husband that similar jewelry was being sold at J.C. Penny's. At that time J.C. Penny's was one of the largest high end retail stores in the United States. Nishioka Shihan went to J.C. Penny's in Honolulu and asked if they would like to sell black coral jewelry. The buyer at J.C. Penny's already had a number of suppliers and, at first, was not interested in more jewelry. Then she saw the piece of jewelry Nishioka Shihan brought with him. The jewelry spoke for itself and the buyer became quite interested in having the store carry this jewelry. The quality and beauty was unique and went on to become a hit, particularly with Japanese and mainland tourists. The number of pieces J.C. Penny's initially wanted was too many for the divers and makers to fulfill; they could only make three a day. So Nishioka Shihan obtained a written purchase order from J.C. Penny's. With this in hand he went to the bank and used it as collateral for a loan which he then invested in developing a much needed business in Maui.

This humble gift started a chain of events that grew into a business providing many jobs to people in Maui and through-

---

22   Slippers are known as flip flops on the mainland.

out the Islands. Because of Nishioka Shihan's concern for the workers, the working and safety conditions improved for the divers, which was a very dangerous job. As the jewelry business grew it eventually expanded to include diamonds and other rare gems but Nishioka Shihan still has the most fondness for the Hawaiian Coral jewelry. Despite this success, Shihan did not become a wealthy business man. Instead, he spread the wealth to others so everyone could have a "comfortable living."

Together, Nishioka Shihan and Mrs. Nishioka ran their family business known as Patmounts. They employed 10 people in the various jobs of mounting jewelry to business office duties. Often, they employed persons with disabilities referred to them from the State and they would extend Christmas bonuses to their employees. These were practices not commonly done at the time. Although Patmounts could have grown into a large corporation they remained a small family business. The Nishioka's goal was to always create a quality item and treat their employees well.

These businesses required frequent trips to Japan which allowed him to continue to train with Kawaguchi Sensei and visit Ohtsuka Sensei and Suzuki Sensei. During one of these trips

Ohtsuka Sensei suggested to Nishioka Shihan that he should be credited with the propagation of Karate in the United States and should consider creating his own school.[23]

In the coming years Nishioka Shihan continued to make frequent trips to eastern Asia, including Okinawa, Vietnam, Taiwan, Korea and Hong Kong to expand his knowledge of martial arts. Nishioka Shihan travelled to Vietnam three times where he studied White Crane Kung Fu and other forms of Kung Fu. While in Taiwan and Hong Kong he expanded his knowledge of these types of Kung Fu. In Korea he observed Tae Kwon Do.

In 1962 he met with Choshin Chibana[24] in Okinawa. He did not train with Chibana, who was 77 years old at that time, but he did learn a great deal about the history and philosophy of Karate. While in Okinawa, Nishioka Shihan also visited and

---

23   The interpretation of "school" at this time was quite different than our present day meaning. At that time school meant Ryu, or loosely interpreted as "style". There is some academic debate as to what is the difference between a Ryu and a Do. Based on his research, Shihan believes there are only two Ryus: Shorin and Goju. He has stated; "If you do the Pinans you are Shorin Ryu. It does not matter which style."

24   Choshin Chibana (1885 -1969) was born in the Shuri district of Okinawa and learned karate from Anko Itosu. He is credited as the farther of modern Kobayashi Style (Small Forest) Shorin Ryu first named in 1928.

observed training conducted by Chibana's student Nakasato Sensei in Naha[25].

Traveling with Nishioka Shihan to Okinawa was one of his top yudansha students from Hawaii, Pat Nakata.[26] Nishioka Shihan asked Chibana if he would take Pat Nakata as a student to mature him in the background of Karate. Chibana accepted and with Shihan's blessing, Pat Nakata remained in Okinawa to continue his training with Choshin Chibana.

Chibana felt that karate's most important lesson was that of humbleness. He would tell Nishioka Shihan the parable of the apple tree: "An apple tree that is full of apples hangs its branches low. So when you are full of knowledge, you bend your head down low." Shihan was impressed by Chibana's knowledge and humbleness and states he was the closest to the reality of what karate really is and how karate came to be.[27]

---

25   Naha is a costal city on the eastern side of the southern island of Okinawa

26   Pat Nakata (10/14/1944 to present) began training with Nishioka Shihan in 1957 at the age of twelve. He was the first student below 18 years of age Shihan accepted to teach. Nakata Sensei currently teaches Shorin-Ryu Karate in Kapahulu, Hawaii and remains in contact with Nishioka Shihan. The name of Pat Nakata's school is the Okinawan Shorin-ryu Karate Association (OSKA) and he was featured in Classical fighting Arts magazine in 2007.

27   Karate Kung Fu Illustrated, May 1988 P. 29

Uchimata throw by Nishioka Shihan at Kodokan Judo Institute, Tokyo, circa 1961

Kodokan Judo Institute Nishioka Shihan performing Pinan Yodan circa 1959

Hironori Ohtsuka (Lt.) and Walter Nishioka (2nd from Lt.) observing class at Tokyo University

Hironori Ohtsuka. Founder of Wado-ryu

Yoshio Kawaguchi Sensei (Lt.) Nishioka Shihan (middle) Ohtsuka Sensei (rt) at Akamon main entrance of Tokyo University

Tournament Ceremony (c. 1961) at the Maritime Hamamatsu AFB in Central Japan. Suzuki Sensei maintained a dojo at the base.

Suzuki demonstrating board breaking at Hamamatsu Maritime Air Force Base.
Nishioka Shihan is one of the board holders.

Japan Air (c. 1961) landing at Hamamatsu Base. Lt. to rt: Pilot, Walter Nishioka,Tatsuo Suzuki, Hironori Ohtsuka and Co-pilot.

Nishioka Shihan with Choshin Chibana at Shuri Hill, Old Capital City of Okinawa, circa 1962. Note the maki-wara board in the background. The sign in the lower left reads: "Shuri Hill, Old Capital City of Okinawa".

Photo of Choshin Chibana (seated) and Pat Nakata (standing). This photo was presented by Pat Nakata to his Sensei, Nishioka Shihan. Written on the photo is " To: Nishioka Sensei" (upper left); "your student, Pat Nakata" (lower right)

Above: Naha Dojo
Left: Nakasato Sensei correcting a student. Nakasato was a student of Chibana. Nishioka Shihan had the opportunity to observe their training.

The Hawaiian Tobiishi

When Nishioka Shihan was not traveling and studying martial arts in Japan and other Asian countries, he was in Hawaii teaching others what he had learned. He began having formal classes early in 1956. Neither the dojo nor the style had a name. His teachings were based on the skills he had learned while in the military. At that time he did not know any katas and had not really had any significant exposure to karate. It was not until his travels to Japan beginning in 1956 that he had more extensive exposure to Karate.

The first named organization occurred in 1958 and was called Hawaii Karate Goshin-Kai. Goshin is interpreted as "self preservation". Other interpretations of goshin are self defense and protector of the spirit. Kai is interpreted as club or association. Loosely interpreted Goshin Kai is "Self Preservation Club". Shortly after this the school name became known as the All Japan Karate League, Hawaii Branch Headquarter. The All Japan Karate League would later become known as Wado-ryu. Goshin Kai became the Hawaiian representative for Japan's Wado Ryu. Walter Nishioka received a certificate from Ohtsuka naming him the Chief Instructor of The All Japan Karate League in Hawaii.

The dojo was located in the Moilili Community Center on S. King Street in Honolulu. The Community Center was also shared with a Jujitsu Dojo. Eventually this building was razed and a traditional dojo was built by Nishioka Shihan in 1960 behind his home in Manoa Valley. This unassuming metal roofed

Moilili Community Center, Goshin Kai Training and Patch. The patch is a white background with black stitching except for the two outer circles and the Japanese Flag which are red. (c. 1957 – 58)

Goshin Kai photos (c. 1958)

Nishioka Shihan demonstrating pivot points.

Stick fighting techniques

Goshin Kai photos (c 1958)

Above: Joseph Kapahu executing tobi yoko geri. Note the background lists jujitsu techniques that were taught in a Jujitsu Dojo that shared the building.

Goshin Kai photos (c. 1958)

Defense against a knife

Goshin Kai photos (c. 1958).

Jujitsu and wrist lock techniques.

Goshin Kai photos (c 1958).

Goshin Kai dojo. Nishioka Shihan is standing in the front row. Note the different training equipment on the floor.

Photo of All Japan Karate League, Hawaii Branch HQ. This was the name of Ohtsuka Sensei's school in Japan before it became known as Wado Ryu. Goshin Kai adopted this name for a short time before Shihan received permission to form his own style. After which the School was named the Statewide Karate Association (SKA).

Nishioka Shihan wearing a Jacket embroidered with "All Japan Karate League - Hawaii Mission" on the breast pocket commemorating the 1961 visit.

All Japan Karate League visiting Hawaii in 1961
Standing Lt. to rt: Tatsuo Suzuki / Nishioka Shihan / Ohtsuka Shihan / Yoshio Kawaguchi / Kiyohisa Hirano
Kneeling Lt. to rt: Jack Matsuda / Kiyoshi Nada

building, slightly larger than a garage, became Honbu[28]. "A Honbu is not only a place to train Karate, but most importantly, a place to plan and control the IKL destiny" .... Nishioka Shihan[29].

In addition to teaching karate, a high school classmate asked Nishioka Shihan if he would become a volunteer civilian instructor at Schofield Army base. The classmate was a Top First Sergeant at Schofield Army Barracks located on Oahu (circa 1964-65). At the Schofield Barracks Nishioka Shihan taught the combat helicopter door gunners, known as "Shotgunners", who were being deployed to Vietnam. He also gave seminars and instruction to the base instructors that taught hand to hand combat to the Army Rangers. Nishioka Shihan taught them hand to hand combat techniques, knife work, Tomiki pivot points and stick techniques.[30]

In 1961 Shihan successfully brought Professor Ohtsuka, Professor Suzuki, Professor Kawaguchi and Kyohisa Hirano for a two month visit to the Hawaiian Islands. At that time Japanese Nationals could only travel in the United States for business and educational reasons. Karate was considered an art by the Department of Immigrations and received the education-

---

28   Headquarters or Main Dojo.

29   From the 2nd annual IKL Newsletter in 1986. Taken from Nishioka Shihan's opening letter to the school.

30   The stick techniques mentioned in this book are not to be confused with the Filipino Escrima stick fighting. These techniques are based on a Japanese fighting technique using a stick similar to an escrima stick but heavier and usually shorter (18 inches).

1965 Karate Congress. Front row (Lt. to rt): James Miyaji, Kenneth Murakami, Robert Igarashi, Winfred Ho
Back row: Mitsugi Kobayashi, Yoshio Murasaki, William Toyofuku, Walter Nishioka, Carlton Shimomi

Note: James Miyaji continues to be a close friend of Nishioka Shihan. He currently is a Sensei of Shorin-ryu karate in Oahu. His school, Kenshukan Karate Club, is part of Nihon Butoku Kai. Through the years Miyaji helped Nishioka Shihan with tournaments, judging and refereeing. They also collaborated on many of the old katas throughout the years. He was President of the Karate Congress and was also past President of the Hawaii Kodansha Association.

al designation. Nishioka Shihan was instrumental in obtaining permission from the Department for their extended stay. He personally vouched for their character and was able to secure the necessary papers for their visit. During their stay in Hawaii they stayed with Nishioka Shihan at his residence in Manoa.

The group toured the islands giving demonstrations and teaching seminars about Wado-Ryu, known at that time as the All Japan Karate League. The previous year Ohtsuka had encouraged Nishioka Shihan to consider starting his own School. After much deliberation and as prescribed by proper etiquette, Nishioka Shihan asked Professor Ohtsuka if it was appropriate for him to start a school (style) of his own. Upon Ohtsuka's return to Japan he replied in a letter: "..... because of the caliber of training you have had in the past... I will give you my blessings..."

During the early 60's Hawaii had a unique martial arts environment that was absent in the rest of the United States. There were many different styles of martial arts in Hawaii primarily because a large portion of Hawaii's population was of Asian heritage. At first this diversity may seem an advantage, but at this time many of the schools still had close ties and governance by the parent organizations in Japan or Okinawa. As a result, cooperation between the different styles was difficult and sometimes discouraged by the parent organization. This made sharing of resources and holding combined tournaments very difficult, especially since there was only one dojo of each style on the Island.

Perhaps due to this martial arts diversity, Hawaii was beginning to see a decline in the practice of martial arts. This result-

All Women's Class (c. 1959). At this time it was socially unacceptable for men to strike at women, even in a martial training environment. Many women wanted to learn martial arts but were concerned about the contact so Nishioka Shihan met their needs by being one of the first martial arts instructors to offer an all women's class.

ed in a novel collaboration in 1959 of six martial arts individuals with a goal "to foster goodwill among the various karate clubs and further the advancement of Karate in Hawaii".[31] This resulted in the formation of the Hawaii Karate Association[32]. The Hawaii Karate Association represented schools from Shorin-ryu, Goju-ryu and Mitase Kenpo.

In 1962 more members were added to bring the membership to nine individuals. Nishioka Shihan was one of these individuals. With the addition of these new members the name was changed to the Hawaii Karate Congress. In 1965 Nishioka Shihan was elected president of the Hawaii Karate Congress and went on to serve a second term as president.

While president, Nishioka Shihan would function as an arbitrator during disputes between different schools or in tournaments. He also introduced the idea of limiting strikes to the body for children participating in tournaments. This practice was not being done anywhere in the country. This idea eventually became popular and is now a common practice in all karate tournaments throughout the country.

With the continued growth of his own School, Nishioka Shihan eventually declined to continue as an active member and diplomatically left the Congress so he could focus his attention

31   Black Belt Magazine, August 1966 James Miyaji

32   The Hawaii Karate Association was created by Paul Yamaguchi, Kenneth Murakami, Mitsugi Kobayashi, George Miyasaki, Carlton Shimomi and James Miyaji.

Statewide Karate League Patch

SKL Hanko

Honbu Dojo (c. Early 1960's). A class was held at 9 a.m. and another at 11 a.m. This photo shows those combined classes. Nishiokas Shihan is at far left.

Honbu shortly after construction located in Nishioka Shihan's backyard at his residence in Manoa Valley. c. 1960

Nishioka Shihan executing Tobi Mae Geri in Honbu.

Honbu shortly after construction. Honbu c. 1960

Recent photo of Honbu

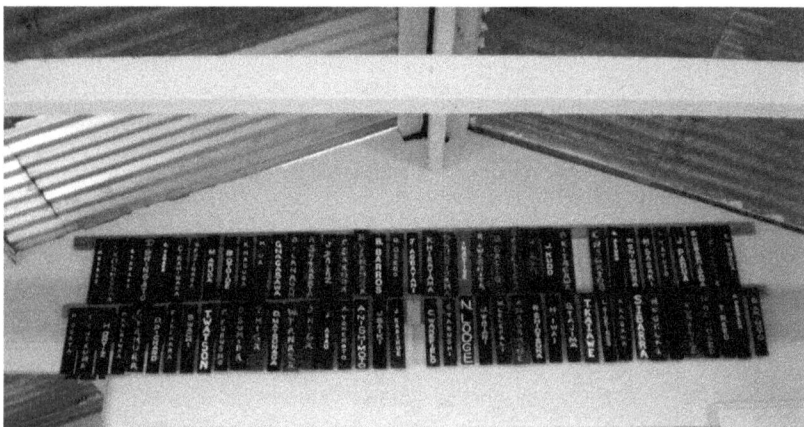

Nafuda Kake hanging in Honbu. Nafuda Kake are wooden name plates of the active yudansha in IKL. The nafuda now occupy space on two walls.

on developing his own school. Nishioka Shihan's school was becoming large enough that the dojos were able to compete against each other in their own tournaments. Many of the martial artist in the Congress would attend Nishioka's tournaments to help judge. They would often comment how his school's karateka were always the most respectful of any students.

When Nishioka Shihan started his own style in 1961 he relinquished his yudansha ranks in all the styles he had trained. He "became" the school and as a result, the source from which all rank in the new school comes forth. At that time he held a Nidan in Judo, a Shodan in Jujitsu and a Nidan in Wado-ryu. This was when Wado-ryu was still on the five Dan system which meant a Nidan ranking was much higher than it is today.

Honbu Shomen. Top row are photos of Shihan's teacher's, honored IKL yudansha and Shihan. Below the top row are photos of the IKL Yudansha that have submitted photos.

The new school created after receiving Ohtsuka's blessing assumed the name Statewide Karate Association in 1963.
An article appeared in a Japanese language periodical in
March 1963, the Hawaii Times, reporting the creation of this
new Karate School named Statewide Karate Association. In
that article he was referred to by the respectful title of "Saiko
Shihan", meaning "Highest Master", "Teacher of High Principles" or "Best Instructor-in-Chief". Nishioka Shihan does
not recall how the title "Shihan" actually started but from that
point on the title of Shihan was used by his students when
they addressed him. Nishioka Shihan notes that rank and titles
mean nothing to him personally but they are important for the
school's students and the functioning of the school.

The name choice of Statewide Karate Association was par-
tially influenced and suggested by Nishiyama Sensei of Shotokan in Japan. Shotokan was also known as Japan Karate Association. Nishioka Shihan had been training with Nishiyama
and as a result used a similar name for his school.

Nishioka Shihan's original thoughts were to have a style
with a judo section (Judo Bu) and a karate section (Karate Bu)
in this new style. The Judo section would incorporate the self
defense techniques he learned in jujitsu and the military. But
realizing this was too much for most individuals to learn, he
decided to focus on Karate Do. The reason Nishioka Shihan decided to focus on Karate and not Judo or self defense is simply
"because you can practice Karate by yourself."

Since Nishioka Shihan received Ohtsuka's blessing to begin
a new School and he decided to focus on Karate, the name was

changed from Statewide Karate Association to Statewide Karate League. Wado-ryu was original named All Japan Karate League. As Nishioka Shihan became closer to Ohtsuka, Kawaguchi and Suzuki Sensei of Wado Ryu, this influenced the choice of changing the name from Association to League.

Banner from SKA. Background is green. This banner is hanging in Honbu. Karate Bu signifies that this banner was going to indicate the Karate Section of SKA

Initially it was considered to name the school "All" State Karate League because in Japan it was "All" Japan Karate League. However, at that time many businesses were using the term "Allstate" such as Allstate Batteries and Allstate Insurance. As a result it was decided to drop the "All" that was typically used in Japanese School names.

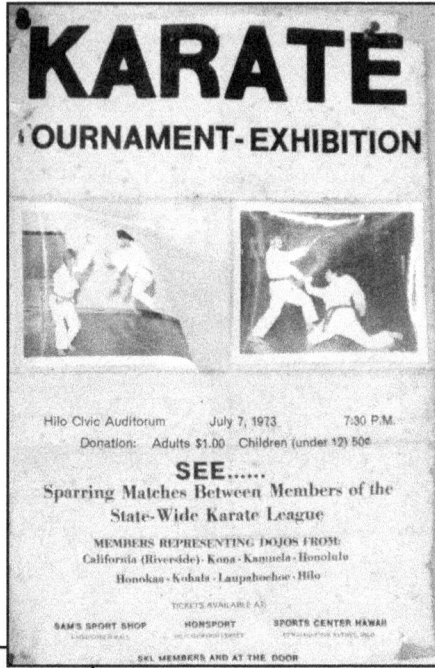

1973 Poster for Hilo
tournament - exhibition

1987 Idaho IKL
Tournament Booklet

SKA Dojo (c. 1966) Front Row Lt. to Rt: Sheldon Kobashigawa, James Kudo, Victor Young, John Balasz. Back Row Lt. to RT: Larry Hator, Howard Ortiz, Mike Visser, Paul, Joe Kahapea, Richard Nakano, Terry Higa

SKL continued as the school's name for 23 years. During that time bylaws and operating manuals were created. A Board of Governors was also created to help manage the school. In 1984 SKL adopted the more common ju-dan black belt ranking which was created by the Kodokan Judo system, over their current godan system. This allowed more accurate comparison of the SKL student's rank to other styles.

By 1986, dojos were started on the mainland so a change in the name was needed. Nishioka elected to change the name to International Karate League (IKL) to accommodate potential future growth. The IKL hanko was registered in Japan.[33] At this time the school was organized into regions. Dojos were opened on Maui and the Big Island of Hawaii. Through IKL students from Honbu and these first dojos, the School spread to California, Minnesota, Utah and Idaho. Currently there are 26 Dojos located throughout these States.

While studying the history of karate, Nishioka Shihan came to the conclusion that if a karate school has Itosu's Pinan Katas then it is Shorin -ryu.[34] With this in mind, he did not feel it was

---

33   A hanko is a stamp, usually carve stone, that is used in lieu of a signature and thus registered to prevent forgery. The hanko insures the authenticity of any Yudansha Certificate issued by IKL.

34   Anko Itosu (1831-1915) is considered by many to be the father of modern karate. He was instrumental in having karate reintroduced to the schools in Okinawa around 1905. He created the five Pinans to teach the school children realizing the older katas were to complicated.

appropriate to use the term Ryu in naming his new School. The definition of Ryu is "a formalized martial tradition".[35] Many believe a ryu is based on a long history, its techniques, and beliefs that are directly related to the training of bushi (warriors). Given this definition, martial arts such as Kendo and Judo would not be considered ryus since they were developed more as sports. Nishioka Shihan believes there are only two general Ryus: Shorin-ryu and Goju-ryu. Shorin-ryu was originally called Shuri-te because of its origins in the Okinawan capital of Shuri. Goju-ryu was originally called Naha-te because it had its origins in the costal Okinawan city of Naha.

Nishioka Shihan applied his outlook and experiences from his military and ongoing travels to the Far East in the creation of this new style. The International Karate League (Kokusai Karate Renmei) is considered a modified Shorin-ryu style. It's Shorin-ryu roots are primarily Wado-ryu with some Shotokan and Shito-ryu[36] influences. It is modified with influences from

---

35 Dictionary of Japanese Martial Arts. Reliance, TN: Yamazato Publications.

36 Shito-ryu was founded by Kenwa Mabuni in 1931. It is consider a combination of karate styles. One element utilizes long stances and physical power such as in Shotokan and Shuri-te styles. While at the same time having characteristics of directional movements, power extended with breathing, and elements of Naha-te and Tomari-te.

Nishioka Shihan's training in Judo, Jujitsu, Aikido[37], White Crane Kung Fu[38], Goju-ryu[39] and his background in military self defense.

---

37   Aikido was founded by Morihei Ueshiba. Often interpreted as "Way of Harmonious Spirit" it incorporates blending with the attacker and redirecting the attacker's energy. Shihan studied under Kenji Tomiki, an early student of Ueshiba. Tomiki (1900 - 1979) was also a judo student of Jigoro Kano. Tomiki went on to be the founder of the Japan Aikido Association (JAA).

38   White Crane Kung Fu is considered to have started in the Fajian Providence of China possibly around 1700's. It is one of the five Chinese boxing systems that developed from observing animals (crane, tiger, snake, dragon and leopard). White Crane incorporates the pecking motion and wing flapping of the white crane.

It's predecessor was introduced to China by the Buddhist monk Sing-Lung, from the Tibetan Hop Gar martial system. Today White Crane is closely associated with Federations in Hong Kong (where Nishioka Shihan studied it) and Singapore. The philosophy of White Crane is the same as Hop Gar's and is based on four words: Chon (to destroy), Sim (to evade), Chun (to penetrate) and Jeet (to intercept).

39   Chojun Miyagi (Okinawan) is considered to be the founder of Goju-ryu. It originated in the Okinawan city of Naha. Gogen Yamaguchi (Japanese) was the founder of the Goju-ryu Karate Association in Tokyo, Japan. Yamaguchi was a student of Miyagi. Literally translated to Hard (Go) and Soft (Ju) style it incorporates strong linear attacks with circular open hand movements. It incorporates a strong emphasis on breathing. Some consider it a descendant of Fujian White Crane from China.

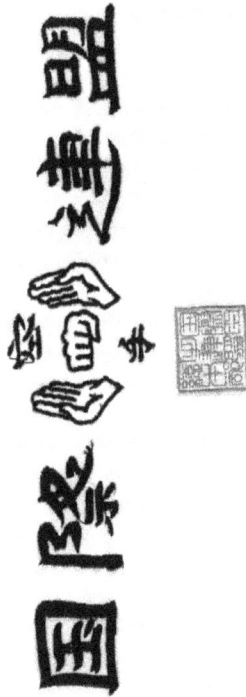

国際合氣連盟

Photo of original IKL Hachi Maki circa 1980's. A hachi maki is a cloth that is folded and used as a head band. The hachi maki pictured above was reproduce by Yudansha Manuel Sanchez for the Y2K tournament and seminar held in Honolulu.

3rd Annual

STATE-WIDE KARATE LEAGUE

CHAMPIONSHIP TOURNAMENT

Sponsored by the EAST MANOA LIONS CLUB

Friday, August 21, 1970 — 8:00 p.m.

MID-PACIFIC INSTITUTE GYMNASIUM

2445 KAALA STREET ● HONOLULU, HAWAII

1970 SKL Tournament program. The photos on the next three pages are taken from this program.

Instructor Richard Nakano Chief Instructor of the Kamuela Waimea, Hawaii Branch applying Elbow Attack on Fred Guzman of California Branch.

Caption reads: Richard Nakano Chief Instructor of the Kamuela Waimea Branch applying Elbow Attack on Fred Guzman of California Branch

SKL Students in Hilo's Japanese Garden (c. 1960's).

Students in Free Fight Training during practice sessions held at HQ of Statewide Karate League, Manoa.

Caption reads: Students in Free Fight Training during practice sessions held at HQ of Statewide Karate League, Manoa.

Sheldon Kobashigawa in a Flying Kick attack toward Fred Guzman of Riverside, California Dojo.

Caption reads; Sheldon Kobashigawa in a Flying Kick attack toward Fred Guzman of Riverside, California Dojo.

Ron Iwata applying a Circle Kick toward Gene Nagasawa as Referee Peter Izutsu calls a full point.

Caption reads: Ron Iwata applying a Circle Kick toward Gene Nagasawa as Referee Peter Izutsu calls a full point.

International Karate League (IKL) Year 2000
Championship Karate Tournament & Convention
Honolulu, Hawaii

2000 IKL Tournament and Convention program

Walter K. Nishioka, Shihan
Japan, 1959

2008
50th Anniversary

2008 50th Anniversary tournament program

Yudansha workout at Shinshu Kyokai Mission Hall during 2000 tournament weekend.

Yudansha present at the 50th Anniversary tournament

Previous IKL Shomen Banner

Current IKL Shomen Banner

IKL Patch

Honolulu Mayor Fasi awarding Nishioka Shihan a "Good Guy" certificate for exhibiting bravery in rescuing a drowning girl on June 9th, 1974.

Nishioka Shihan was at Ala Moana Beach with his children when he heard someone screaming for help. He noticed two young girls drowning in the ocean. He dove in and rescued one of the girls and resuscitated her when they reached the shore.

The girl was living in Honolulu with her parents and sister. Unfortunately her sister, who was swimming with her, was not rescued in time by other bystanders . The sister who survived now lives in California and still visits Nishioka Shihan when she comes to Hawaii.

Nishioka Shihan demonstrating self defense on Wayne Okamura. c. 1990

Nishioka Shihan observing training at Honbu. This photo appeared in the *Hawaii Herald* on Friday, February 6, 1987. Written by Wayne Muromoto.

Nishioka Shihan Demonstrating a technique to Yudansha during seminar on the Big Island in 2010.
Nishioka Shihan was 77 years old when this photo was taken.

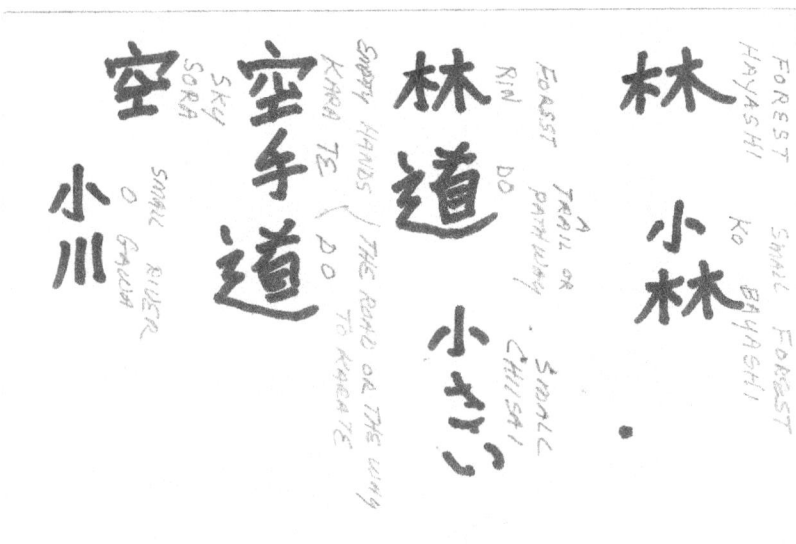

Nishioka Shihan's handwritten explanation of various kanji pertinent to Karate

Rare "unapproved" patches. The upper patch was not approved because of "I.S.K.L". If the "I" was not present it would have been allowed but the placement of the "I" implies a different School. The lower patch was not approved because its color is blue.

Approved outer wear patch design by General Ishimoto. The background is green. General Arthur Ishimoto was a student of Nishioka Shihan who was assigned to Army Military Intelligence in the Hawaii Army National Guard.

Approved outerwear patch commemorating the 50th Anniversary. Original design by Nishioka Shihan and Yudansha Glen Fujinaga. Patch created by Yudansha Robert Rudeen.

Front Row Lt. to Rt: Hanshi James Miyaji - Kenshukan Butokukai Karate Association. Walter Nishioka Shihan. Back Row Lt. to Rt: Sensei Patrick Nakata - Okinawa Shorin Karate Association, Sensei Charles Goodin - Hikari Dojo, Kishaba Juku Shorin Ryu; contributing editor to *Classical Fighting Arts*; creator and founder of the Hawaii Karate Museum located in Hamilton Library on the Manoa Campus of the University of Hawaii.

The Tobiishi Not Taken

"You can only serve one master." ....
Walter Nishioka

Occasionally individuals are in a position in their life where if they make a different decision, or take advantage (or not) of opportunities their lives would turn out quite differently. This was the case with Nishioka Shihan.

Nishioka Shihan never anticipated opportunities would lead him along the path he had taken. When he was young he never dreamed of creating a new style of Karate with a School that would directly and indirectly influence thousands of individuals. In fact his childhood dream was quite different. He was presented opportunities in his life that could have resulted in him following different paths.

Musical Tobiishi

As a teenager, Walter Nishioka had a passion and talent for music. He was considering a musical career and the possibility of studying music in Japan. His hope was to be accepted to study under Masao Koga[40], a famous composer and pioneer of Japanese popular music.

During these teen years Walter Nishioka was very involved in music. He was a talented singer and played a number of instruments including the trumpet, mandolin, ukulele and the shamisen.[41] He had his own small orchestra named The Tsubaki Orchestra and a band named Holo Holo;[42] both played Japanese Music.

Geisha playing a shamisen

---

40   Masao Koga (November 18, 1904 to July 25th, 1978) was a famous Japanese composer who was considered the pioneer of Japanese popular music and the creation of a new genre called enka. The Koga Masao Museum of Music is in Shibuya, Japan.

41   The shamisen is a traditional Japanese instrument with three strings. It is similar in length to a guitar but slimmer and no frets.

42   Holo Holo is a pidgin term for "to go out, as for leisure". The Holo Holo band's members were all students of martial arts.

The Tsubaki Orchestra and Holo Holo band would play at teahouses, weddings and large parties. They would also play for fund raisers, many of which were to raise money to help build churches and temples. Occasionally, Walter Nishioka would stop at different night clubs on the way home from other performances to play with the performing musicians.

In addition to his own band and orchestra Walter Nishioka was invited to perform in the Kotobuke Orchestra on Oahu. The Kotobuke Orchestra was a junior orchestra conducted by the famous Francis Zanami. Francis Zanami was a composer and conductor of the professional Shochiku Orchestra of Honolulu. These Orchestras combined singers and instruments in their performances. This gave Nishioka Shihan opportunities to meet many of the famous singers and performers from Japan.

Walter Nishioka playing the mandolin (center) at Club Ginza, 1951 with Holo Holo. This was his going away party before entering the Air Force.

Tsubaki Orchestra playing at the sound stage at KTOH radio station at Lihue, Kauai in 1950. Nishioka Shihan is seated on the left with the mandolin in the front row.

Holo Holo Band playing at Natsunoya Tea House Garden in Alewa Heights, Honolulu in 1960. Nishioka Shihan is seated third from the right.

98

Performance of the "Four Chosen Orchestras" at McKinley High School in 1949. Conductor is Francis Zanami. Nishioka Shihan's orchestra, Tsubaki, is on the right with him seated in the seat on the left.

Nishioka Shihan with Japan's top singers and Shamisen legend. Left to right: Sato Keiko, Shamisen legend, Kouta Katsutaro, Walter Nishioka, Watanabe Hamako. 1949

When Walter Nishioka graduated from high school and volunteered for active duty in the Air Force, his musical interests travelled with him. While at Lowry Air Force base in Denver in 1952 he became a member of the Mile High Band. The Mile High Band would play jazz-like music in J-town.[43] Walter Nishioka played the shamisen and ukulele. He was well know for his performance of "Shamisen Bogey", a well known song from 1950 that was popularized by Japanese singers from Japan and Hawaii.

During his visits to J-town he developed ongoing ties with a family that lived there. The family that befriended Nishioka Shihan also befriended another Hawaiian serviceman named George Naope. Through this mutual adoptive family Walter Nishioka became acquainted with George Naope and played music with him in J-town. George Naope went on to become the founder of Hawaii's Merrie Monarch Festival in 1964.[44]

Music continued to be a presence in Walter Nishioka's life after returning from the military. When he began Goshin Kai in the 50's a security guard, Charles Kalani, at the Hawaiian Hilton Village in Waikiki became Nishioka Shihan's karate

---

43   J-town was terminology used at the time to identify parts of a city that was predominately occupied by Japanese Americans.

44   George Naope (2/25/1928 - 10/26/09) founded The Merrie Monarch Festival which is a week long festival of traditional Hawaiian arts, crafts and performances featuring a three day Hula competition. The festival is still held annually in Hilo, Hawaii.

student. A famous Hawaiian musician, Arthur Lyman,[45] was performing at the Hawaiian Hilton and Charles Kalani was in the security detail to provide protection. Arthur Lyman wanted to learn the same karate Charles knew so Charles Kalani introduced him to Nishioka Shihan. Arthur Lyman became a student of Nishioka Shihan's (at that time is was SKL).

Walter Nishioka continued to play recreational music and still had a small orchestra. Many of the members of his orchestra were also his karate students. They would often travel to give Karate demonstrations on the neighboring islands and during intermission change from their karate gi and perform music, much to the surprise and joy of the spectators.

Nishioka Shihan also participated, and won, in karaoke competitions. To this day he still exercises his voice at a Honolulu karaoke club.

---

45   Arthur Lyman (2/2/32 - 2/24/02) was known as "The King of Lounge Music". Arthur Lyman went on to become one of Hawaii's most famous recording artists. He recorded 30 albums, 400 singles and had three gold albums.

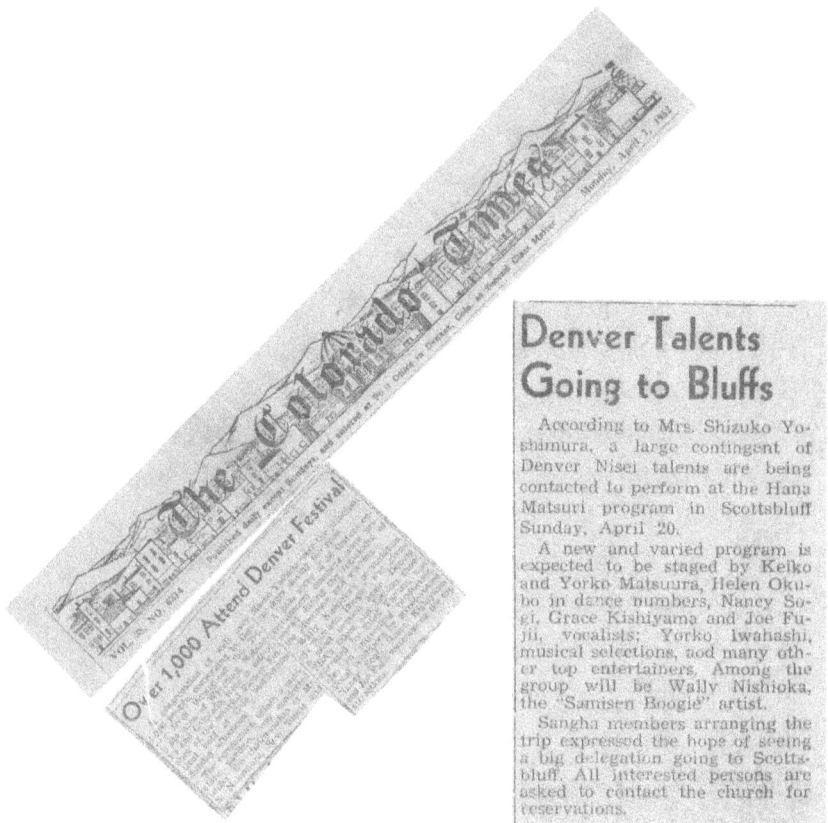

Denver Talents Going to Bluffs

According to Mrs. Shizuko Yoshimura, a large contingent of Denver Nisei talents are being contacted to perform at the Hana Matsuri program in Scottsbluff Sunday, April 20.

A new and varied program is expected to be staged by Keiko and Yorko Matsuura, Helen Okubo in dance numbers, Nancy Sogi, Grace Kishiyama and Joe Fujii, vocalists; Yorko Iwahashi, musical selections, and many other top entertainers. Among the group will be Wally Nishioka, the "Samisen Boogie" artist.

Sangha members arranging the trip expressed the hope of seeing a big delegation going to Scottsbluff. All interested persons are asked to contact the church for reservations.

Articles appearing in Colorado Newspapers (1952):

Excerpt from left reads: "Walter Nishioka presentation of "Shamisen Boogie" was given a great ovation again."

Excerpt from right: ".....among the group will be Wally Nishioka, the "samisen boogie" artist."

Above: Nishioka Shihan (right) playing Mandolin with George Naope in the Mile High Band in J-town at the Cherry Blossom Festival in 1952.

Right: Nishioka Shihan playing Ukulele solo at the Festival.

Nishioka Shihan singing at a 1987 event.

Nishioka Shihan exercising his voice at a Honolulu Karaoke Club, 2011.

Hollywood Tobiishi

Another possible path Nishioka Shihan could have taken presented itself after he was beginning to establish his own School in Hawaii. Martial arts was gaining popularity through television shows such as the Green Hornet and Bruce Lee movies. Many Hollywood stars began taking martial arts at this time but there were few qualified teachers in California. One qualified instructor was Ed Parker[46], founder of American Kenpo Karate. Mr. Parker, who was born in Hawaii, would make frequent trips to Hawaii. On two of these occasions he visited Nishioka Shihan to encourage him to return with him to California to teach the stars. During one of these visits Ed Parker brought Elvis Presley to Honbu to meet Nishioka Shihan. Another star that visited Nishioka Shihan at Honbu was Ricardo Montalban.

Nishioka Shihan humbly declined Mr. Parker's encouragement. Nishioka Shihan's personal feeling was to keep commercialism out of his School. As always, he just wanted to focus on learning and teaching karate. He was concerned commercialism would distract him from this objective.

---

46   Ed Parker (3/19/1931 to 12/15/1990) trained in judo and the Kenpo under Frank Chow. He went on to form the American Kenpo Karate which later became International Kenpo Karate Association.

Tobiishi and the Do of IKL

A Japanese strolling garden (Kaiyu-shiki) requires a participant to walk through the garden, following the tobiishi (stepping stones 飛石) offered to him, to be fully appreciated. It is up to the individual to discover what the garden has to offer. And to fully appreciate the garden you must participate in the surroundings and the tempo of the garden; not just be a casual observer.

In a kaiyu-shiki some tobiishi are set irregularly, forcing the individual to look down to avoid tripping. This may show the participant something they may have otherwise missed or cause them to divert their glance just long enough so that when they look back up they are greeted by an unexpected surprise that the garden reveals. In some parts of the garden the tobiishi follow a straight path and allow a quick passage while others follow a winding course, forcing the participant to slow their pace and understand what the garden has to offer. The over all "hide and reveal" purpose of the garden is meant to enlighten and revive the spirit of the participant.

Nishioka Shihan is walking a similar path through his life and his participation in karate. He has taken a very difficult path of dedication and sacrifice that many of us are unable to make.

He has followed a path that has presented many opportunities. Some of these opportunities would have led him down different paths. Fortunately for IKL karateka and the martial arts world he choose the path he did.

This path was not easy for Nishioka Shihan. It was a difficult path that many are unwilling to make. The circumstances of the era made his Asian travels even more admirable. The long hours of training and the pursuit of unattainable perfection of an art has not wavered over six decades. All the while he has maintained the integrity established by the masters that preceded him.

Many steps along this path were anticipated, some were not. Some were easy and others presented tribulations that most would have abandon the path. But with each tobiishi along the way he has experienced and learned the nature of karate and in his teachings and by example he has given us the opportunity to share those experiences. He has laid the tobiishi of his path (Do) for us to choose to follow. It is up to us to participate and learn.

"The essence of a Japanese garden is only complete when it is understood...." Unknown

Time Line Nishioka Shihan

Walter Nishioka
Birth date June 18, 1932
Kalihi district Honolulu

1941-1951- Trained with Henry Seishiro Okazaki and his disciples in Judo, Jujitsu, Karate, Yawara, Stick Fighting & Kendo
1948 - Received Shodan in Jujitsu from Okazaki
1949 – Joins Naval Reserves
1950 – Graduates from High School

1951
- Volunteered for the US Air Force
- Received honorable discharge from Naval Reserves

1952
- Became instructor at survival training camp at the request of Sgt. John Hodges.
- Later became head instructor when Hodges transferred to Washington, DC

1953
- He trained and coached the championship judo team at Walker Air Force Base.
- The team won the 8th air force championship.

Next page

1953 Strategic Air Command Tour
- Ohtake-sensei: Judo (locks, restraints, strangle holds)
- Sato-sensei: tachiwaza (judo: catches opponent off balance)
- Tomiki-sensei: Aikido
- Hosokawa-sensei: disarming techniques (judo)
- Nishiyama-sensei: Shotokan karate
- Kamada-sensei: Shotokan karate
- Obata-sensei: Shotokan karate
- Kobayashi – sensei: Judo
- Kotani sensei: Judo
- Ishikawa sensei: Judo

1954
- Trained under Captain "Red" Purvis in the art of knife combat while making training films at Paramount Studio in NY and Tampa

1955
- Honorable discharge from Air Force

1957-61
- Goshin Kai (Self Preservation) started (Moilili Community Center)

Next page

1959
- Studied at the Kodokan Judo College
- (Kotani, Ikeda, Ohtake & Hosokawa)
- Earned Shodan Black Belt in Judo (Later received Nidan in 1962)

1959 - onward
- Nishiyama: Karate (Shotokan)
- Trained with Tomiki Sensei
- Introduced to Wado Ryu Style
- Studied Wado Ryu with Kawaguchi, Ohtsuka and Suzuki
- Yamaguchi Gogen: Goju Ryu
- Studied Shito Ryu

1960
- Honbu built
- Received Shodan from Ohtsuka in Wado Ryu

1961
- Brought Ohtsuka, Suzuki, Kawaguchi and Hirano to Hawaii
- School known as All Japan Karate League, Hawaii Headquarters.
- Received permission to create own style from Ohtsuka

Next page

1962- onward
- Earned Nidan in Wado ryu based on Godan grading system (1962)
- Visits Okinawa: Choshin Chibana: Karate (Shorin Ryu)
- Visits Korea - Observes Tae Kwon Do
- Visits Taiwan, Hong Kong, and Viet Nam and studies White Crane Kung Fu and other styles of Kung Fu.

March 1963
- Statewide Karate Association created then changed to Statewide Karate League in 1965

January 1, 1986
- International Karate League created (Kokusai Karate Renmei)

Genealogy of IKL

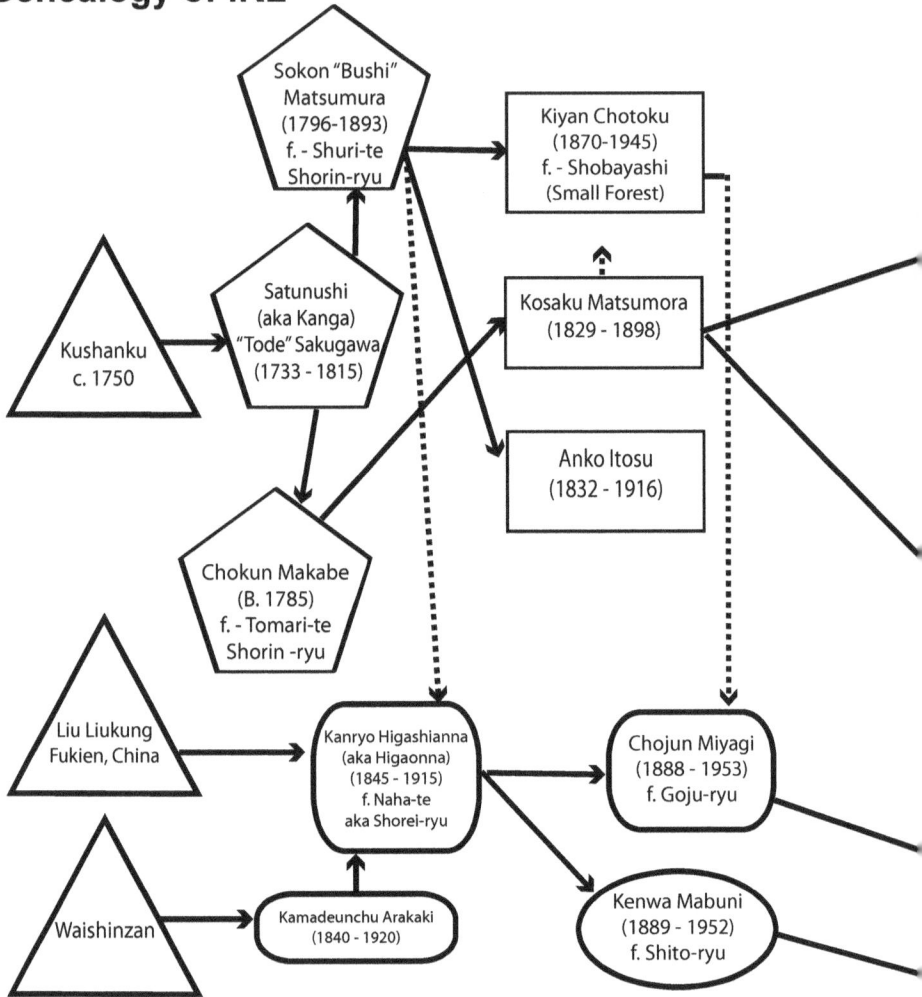

Sokon "Bushi" Matsumura
(1796-1893)
f. - Shuri-te
Shorin-ryu

Kiyan Chotoku
(1870-1945)
f. - Shobayashi
(Small Forest)

Kushanku
c. 1750

Satunushi
(aka Kanga)
"Tode" Sakugawa
(1733 - 1815)

Kosaku Matsumora
(1829 - 1898)

Anko Itosu
(1832 - 1916)

Chokun Makabe
(B. 1785)
f. - Tomari-te
Shorin -ryu

Liu Liukung
Fukien, China

Kanryo Higashianna
(aka Higaonna)
(1845 - 1915)
f. Naha-te
aka Shorei-ryu

Chojun Miyagi
(1888 - 1953)
f. Goju-ryu

Waishinzan

Kamadeunchu Arakaki
(1840 - 1920)

Kenwa Mabuni
(1889 - 1952)
f. Shito-ryu

Legend

△ China influence	◯ Shito-ryu influence	▷ Primary Karate Influence
▢ Shorin-ryu influence	⬡ Other influence	→ Directly trained under
⬠ Credited for Okinawan propagation of karate	◯ Naha-te / Goju-ryu influence	···▷ Indirectly trained under
		⟹ Research, Historic and Philosophical influence
		f. Founder of School

118

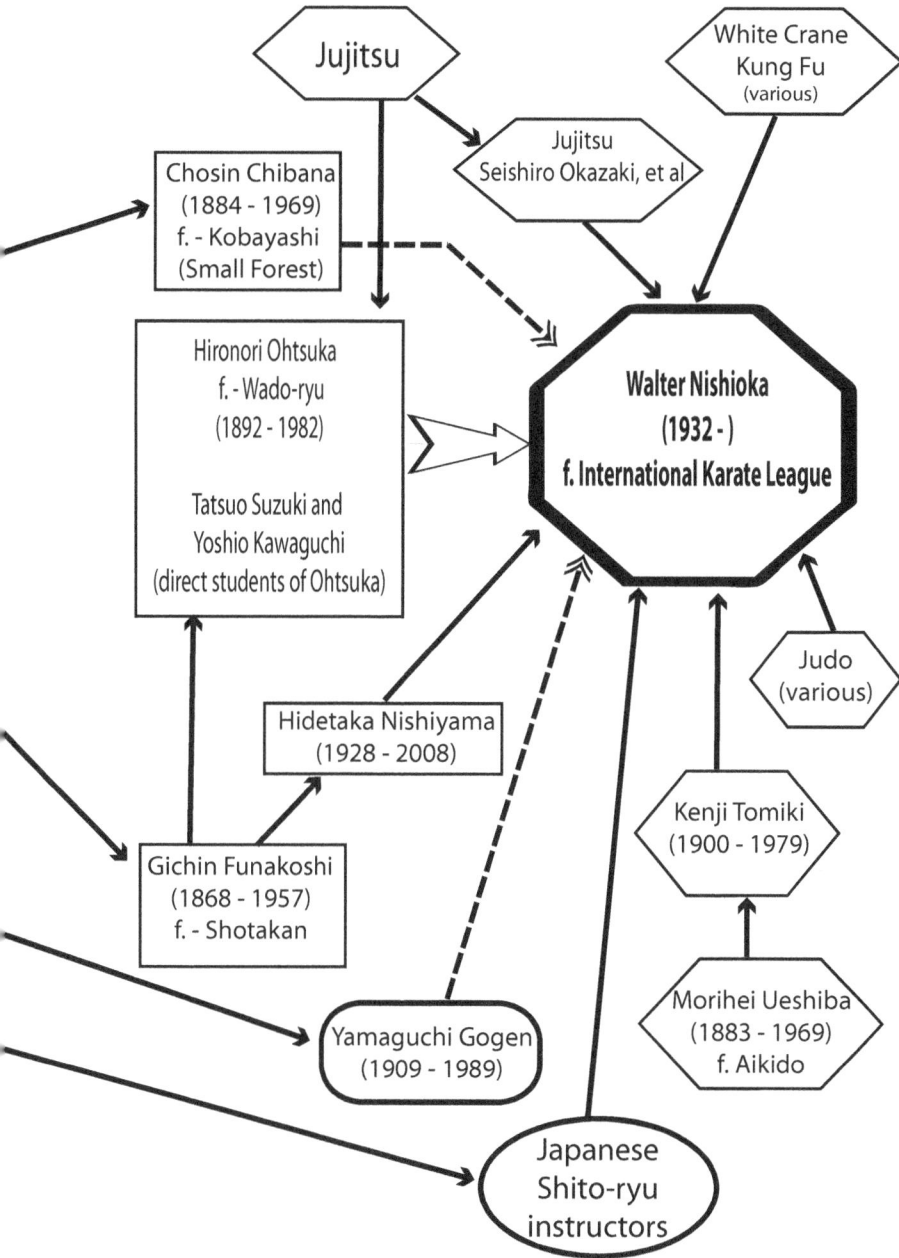

Jujitsu

White Crane
Kung Fu
(various)

Jujitsu
Seishiro Okazaki, et al

Chosin Chibana
(1884 - 1969)
f. - Kobayashi
(Small Forest)

Hironori Ohtsuka
f. - Wado-ryu
(1892 - 1982)

Tatsuo Suzuki and
Yoshio Kawaguchi
(direct students of Ohtsuka)

Walter Nishioka

(1932 -)

f. International Karate League

Hidetaka Nishiyama
(1928 - 2008)

Judo
(various)

Gichin Funakoshi
(1868 - 1957)
f. - Shotakan

Kenji Tomiki
(1900 - 1979)

Yamaguchi Gogen
(1909 - 1989)

Morihei Ueshiba
(1883 - 1969)
f. Aikido

Japanese
Shito-ryu
instructors

These hang in Honbu.

The item on the left is a presentation from Kanazawa's Shoto-kan Hawaii Headquarters in appreciation of IKL karateka's participation and officiating of matches; and Shihan's assistance in officiating and judging in their tournament.

The middle plaque is from Hanshi Gaspar of the Kenjutsuryu Karate Federation in California. Nishioka Shihan promised the founder of Kenjutsuryu, O'Sensei Adlawan, that he would assist Hanshi Gaspar with any matters. Kenjutsuryu continues to have a close relationship with IKL.

The plaque on the right was a gift of appreciation from Mike Visser, a police chief in California. Visser and others were IKL students that went on to create USKO (United States karate Organization) in California.

Honolulu Mayor Fasi awarding Nishioka Shihan a "Good Guy" certificate for exhibiting bravery in rescuing a drowning girl on June 9th, 1974.

Nishioka Shihan was at Ala Moana Beach with his children when he heard someone screaming for help. He noticed two young girls drowning in the ocean. He dove in and rescued one of the girls and resuscitated her when they reached the shore.

The girl was living in Honolulu with her parents and sister. Unfortunately her sister, who was swimming with her, was not rescued in time by other bystanders . The sister who survived now lives in California and still visits Nishioka Shihan when she comes to Hawaii.

DANIEL K. INOUYE
HAWAII

United States Senate
WASHINGTON, DC 20510

July 12, 2008

The International Karate League
50th Anniversary
Honolulu, Hawaii

Dear Friends:

It is my pleasure to welcome all those gathered today on the occasion of the
50th Anniversary of the International Karate League.

The most important reason for this celebration is to honor your Founder and
Chief Instructor, Walter Kenmotsu Nishioka. Without his commitment to
create a lasting martial art organization, the International Karate League
would not be in existence. Nishioka Shihan has been devoted over the years
to continually improve the Karate techniques being taught to his students. His
teachings build inner strength in an individual and develop mental, spiritual and
physical discipline to be able to excel in the art of self-defense, and beyond into
the greater community.

May this surprise gathering be a most memorable one.

Aloha,

DANIEL K. INOUYE
United States Senator

The documents on pages 121 - 126 were presented to Nishioka
Shihan by different legislative bodies on the 50th Anniversary
of his teaching Karate in Hawaii in 2008.
The letter of recognition pictured above is from US Senator
Daniel Inouye.

The Senate

RECOGNIZES AND CONGRATULATES

WALTER KENMOTSU NISHIOKA
FOR HIS DEDICATION TO THE MARTIAL ART OF KARATE IN HAWAII

WALTER KENMOTSU NISHIOKA, is the founder and chief instructor of The International Karate League and is respectfully referred to as Nishioka Shihan by his students. "Shihan" is the chief, the fountainhead of all attributes and the source of the system, from whom all rank originates.

In the 1950s, Nishioka Shihan served in the United States Air Force and because of his prowess at unarmed combat, was transferred to be an instructor of its Survival Training Course. He eventually became the head instructor and has taught over ten thousand trainees hand-to-hand combat techniques. The curriculum he developed included the use of knives or bayonets, billy clubs, pistols, and a multitude of jujitsu techniques.

In 1955, Nishioka Shihan opened Hawaii Karate Goshin-Kai, a self-defense school at the Moiliili Community Center in Honolulu and, in 1960 moved the school to a traditional dojo located behind his home in Manoa Valley. From 1961 through 1965, he visited Okinawa to study the roots of karate and research the Shorin style of karate. In March 1963, he introduced a new school of karate called the Statewide Karate League, a modified Shorin-ryu style of karate with Chinese martial arts modifications.

Under Nishioka Shihan's guidance, dedication, and tutelage, The International Karate League was founded on January 1, 1986, and has grown nationwide with major dojos in Hawaii, California, Minnesota, Idaho, and Utah.

The Senate of the Twenty-Fourth Legislature of the State of Hawai'i, Regular Session of 2008, hereby recognizes and congratulates WALTER KENMOTSU NISHIOKA for his many years of dedication to the martial art of karate in Hawai'i.

Done this __24th__ day of __April 2008__
State Capitol, Honolulu, Hawai'i

The 24th Legislature
Certificate No. 607

Recognition letter from the State of Hawaii Senate

The House of Representatives
State of Hawaii

hereby presents this certificate to

WALTER KENMOTSU NISHIOKA
50ᵀᴴ ANNIVERSARY OF THE INTERNATIONAL KARATE LEAGUE

WHEREAS, WALTER KENMOTSU NISHIOKA, respectfully referred to as Nishioka Shihan by his students, is the founder and chief instructor of the International Karate League; and

WHEREAS, during the past 60 years, NISHIOKA SHIHAN has been instrumental in developing, teaching, and cultivating the martial art of Karate; and

WHEREAS, early in his karate career, NISHIOKA SHIHAN served as the head instructor of the United States Air Force Survival Training School teaching over ten thousand trainees hand-to-hand combat techniques; and

WHEREAS, the survival training school curriculum NISHIOKA SHIHAN taught included the use of knives or bayonets, billy clubs, pistols, and a multitude of survival techniques; and

WHEREAS, in 1956, NISHIOKA SHIHAN opened Hawaii Karate Center as a self-defense school at the Medalli Community Center in Honolulu; and

WHEREAS, in March of 1961, NISHIOKA SHIHAN introduced a new school of Karate, called the Shorin-ji Karate League, a modified Shorin-ryu style of Karate, an Chinese martial art combination; and

WHEREAS, under NISHIOKA SHIHAN's guidance, dedication, and tutelage, The International Karate League was founded on January 1, 1961 and has grown into multiple schools in Hawaii, California, Minnesota, Texas, and Utah; now, therefore,

BE IT RESOLVED by the House of Representatives of the Twenty-fourth Legislature of the State of Hawaii, Regular Session of 2008, that this body hereby recognizes WALTER KENMOTSU NISHIOKA for his many years of dedication to the martial art of Karate in Hawaii, congratulates him on the 50ᵗʰ anniversary of the International Karate League, and extends to him its warmest wishes and best wishes for his continued success in all future endeavors.

Recognition letter from the State of Hawaii House of Representatives

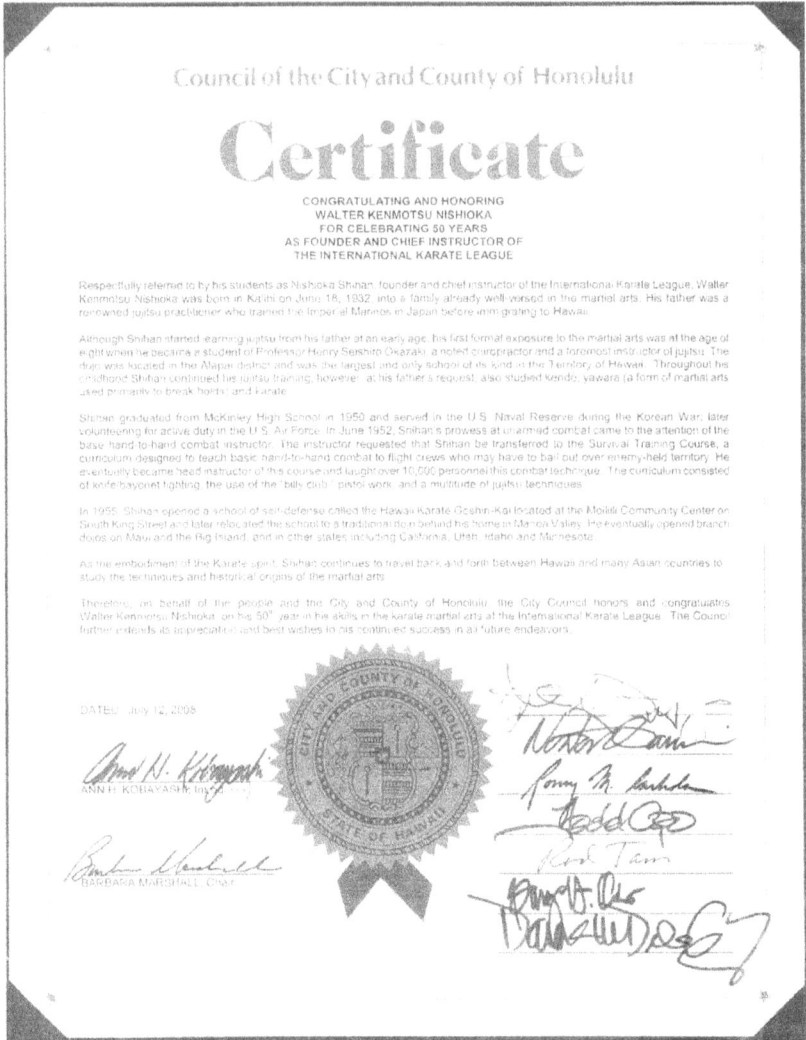

Recognition letter from the Honolulu Council Members

Mayor's Award of Recognition

Shihan Walter Kenmotsu Nishioka

In honor of your 50th anniversary as the founder of the International Karate League and in appreciation for your steadfast and dedicated leadership of this outstanding karate school and your enduring contributions to karate.

Mufi Hannemann
Mayor of Honolulu

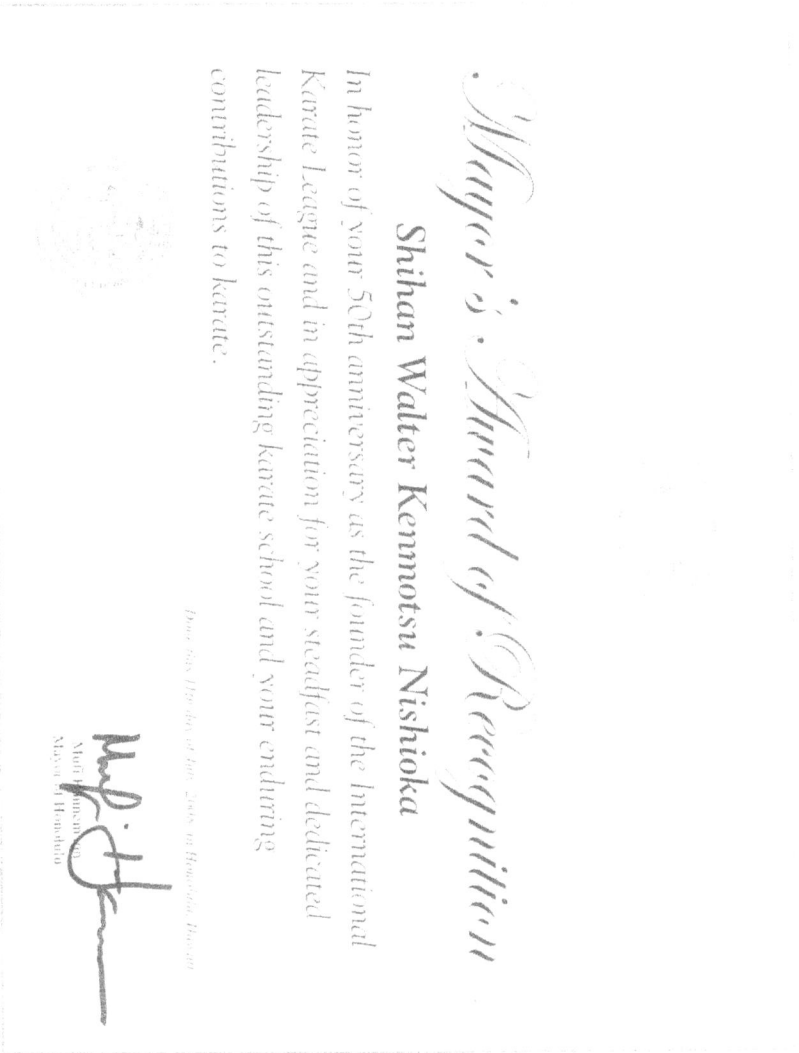

Recognition certificate from Honolulu Mayor Mufi Hannemann

Proclamation

The International Karate League (IKL) or Kokusai Karate Renmei has provided quality karate instruction to Honolulu residents for 50 years. Built by IKL founder and chief instructor Walter Kenmotsu Nishioka in 1958, IKL teaches a modified Shorin-Ryu style of karate. By teaching the practice of karate, as well as developing positive character traits in students, the IKL contributes to the greater community. Since its opening, the IKL has extended its reach, opening schools on the mainland in Idaho, Minnesota and California.

Students of the IKL have the goal of becoming useful and outstanding members of our community, and refine their personal attributes through the rigorous practice of martial arts, namely karate. Karate promotes discipline as well as physical and mental wellness and has deep cultural roots in Japan, where the art form originated. As such, karate also enriches our community through its cultural ties and extensive history.

Respectfully referred to as Nishioka Shihan by his students, this master instructor teaches the karate spirit with his energy, enthusiasm and devotion to the art. He has inspired students over the years to practice the IKL values of faithfulness, respect, effort and etiquette. This year, the IKL honors Nishioka Shihan as they celebrate the 50th anniversary of their school throughout Hawai'i and the mainland. There will also be a tournament showcasing the art form of karate, through which Shihan continues to build strong character, students and community.

THEREFORE, I, LINDA LINGLE, Governor, and I, JAMES R. "DUKE" AIONA, JR., Lieutenant Governor of the State of Hawai'i, do hereby proclaim July 12, 2008 as

INTERNATIONAL KARATE LEAGUE DAY

in Hawai'i, and recognize the accomplishments of Nishioka Shihan.

DONE at the State Capitol, in the Executive Chambers, Honolulu, State of Hawai'i, this twenty-fifth day of June 2008.

Linda Lingle
Governor, State of Hawai'i

James R. "Duke" Aiona, Jr.
Lieutenant Governor, State of Hawai'i

A proclamation from Governor Linda Lingle and Lieutenant Governor Duke Aiona proclaiming July 12, 2008 as International Karate League Day.

Bibliography

Alexander, George W. (1998). Okinawa Island of Karate. Lakeworth, Florida: Yamazoto Publications.

Alexander, George W.; Jespersen, Bo M. (2002). Dictionary of Japanese Martial Arts. Reliance TN: Yamazoto Publications.

Arthur Lyman. (2010, December 24). In Wikipedia, The Free Encyclopedia. Retrieved 02:40, March 16, 2011, from http://en.wikipedia.org/w/index.php?title=Arthur_Lyman&oldid=404001948

Chōshin Chibana. (2011, March 20). In Wikipedia, The Free Encyclopedia. Retrieved 01:50, May 26, 2011, from http://en.wikipedia.org/w/index.php?title=Ch%C5%8Dshin_Chibana&oldid=419884875

Goodin, Charles C. The Hawaii Karate Seinenkai Salutes walter Nishioka. Retrieved August 24, 2008, from Hawaii Karate Seinenkai Web site: http://www.seinenkai.com/

Corcran, John; Farkas, Emil & Sobel, Stuart (Eds.). (1993). The Original Martial Arts Encyclopedia. Los Angeles, CA: Pro-action Publishing.

Ed Parker. (2011, March 7). In Wikipedia, The Free Encyclopedia. Retrieved 02:39, March 16, 2011, from http://en.wikipedia.org/w/index.php?title=Ed_Parker&oldid=417676999

George Na'ope. (2010, November 24). In Wikipedia, The Free Encyclopedia. Retrieved 02:40, March 16, 2011, from http://en.wikipedia.org/w/index.php?title=George_Na%27ope&oldid=398588280

Hara, Jeff. (2004) Interview with Nishioka Shihan that was to be published in Furyu but magazine went out of business prior to publication.

Katsutaro Kouta. (2010, November 27). In Wikipedia, The Free Encyclopedia. Retrieved 01:44, May 26, 2011, from http://en.wikipedia.org/w/index.php?title=Katsutaro_Kouta&oldid=399139621

Keating, Micheline Airman Learn Judo Tactics. Japanese Experts On Tour Teaching 'Art of Gentleness'. (June 27,1953). Tucson Daily Citizen, p. 4.

Muromoto, Wayne What is a Ryu?. Furyu The Budo Journal, Issue 8

Muromoto, Wayne (May 1988). Hawaii's Karate Pioneer Walter Nishioka. Karate Kung-Fu Illustrated, 28-31.

Morihei Ueshiba. (2011, May 23). In Wikipedia, The Free Encyclopedia. Retrieved 01:53, May 26, 2011, from http://en.wikipedia.org/w/index. php?title=Morihei_Ueshiba&oldid=430507469

Nishioka, Walter; personal communication, 1997 - 2011

Noble, Graham, & Goodin, Charles. A Karate Odyssey, an Interview With Sensei Pat Nakata. Classical Fighting Arts, 2(12), 26-32.

Steinhoff, Whitney (2001). Retrieved August 24, 2008, from 1955 Was The Year Web site: http://www.maple-valley.k12.ia.us/HTMLpages/MVSD/ alumni/c1955a/year.html

Suzuki, Tatsuo (2005). My Life. Retrieved August 24, 2008, from Wado International Karate-Do Federation Web site: http://www.wikf.com/mylife. htm

Teshima, Melvin (Ed.). (2004). IKL Manual Section 9.

Various (Authors). International Karate League History. Retrieved August 24, 2008, from IKL.org Web site: http://www.ikl.org/html/iklhistory.html

Background essay: Japanese History A Timeline. Retrieved August 24, 2008, from AskAsia.org Web site: http://www.askasia.org/teachers/essays/ essay.php?no=131&era=&grade=&geo=

Grand Master Hironori Otsuka. Retrieved August 24, 2008, from Wado Karate association of Canada Web site: http://www.wado-kai.com/grand.html

Hidetaka Nishiyama. (2008, July 17). In Wikipedia, The Free Encyclopedia. Retrieved 03:33, August 25, 2008, from http://en.wikipedia.org/w/index. php?title=Hidetaka_Nishiyama&oldid=226283952

Hironori Ōtsuka. (2008, May 23). In Wikipedia, The Free Encyclopedia. Retrieved 02:54, August 25, 2008, from http://en.wikipedia.org/w/index.php ?title=Hironori_%C5%8Ctsuka&oldid=214357218

Japanese garden. (2008, August 20). In Wikipedia, The Free Encyclopedia. Retrieved 03:43, August 25, 2008, from http://en.wikipedia.org/w/index. php?title=Japanese_garden&oldid=233140292

Katsutaro Kouta. (2010, November 27). In Wikipedia, The Free Encyclopedia. Retrieved 02:36, March 16, 2011, from http://en.wikipedia.org/w/index.php?title=Katsutaro_Kouta&oldid=399139621

Kenji Tomiki. Retrieved August 24, 2008, from Wikipedia, the Free Encyclopedia Web site: http://en.wikipedia.org/wiki/Kenji_Tomiki

Korean War. (2008, August 21). In Wikipedia, The Free Encyclopedia. Retrieved 02:52, August 25, 2008, from http://en.wikipedia.org/w/index.php?title=Korean_War&oldid=233255358

Major Events of 1955. Retrieved August 24, 2008, from History Central Web site: http://www.multieducator.com/20th/1955.html

Masao Koga. (2011, January 17). In Wikipedia, The Free Encyclopedia. Retrieved 02:43, March 16, 2011, from http://en.wikipedia.org/w/index.php?title=Masao_Koga&oldid=408357136

Miyahira, Katsuya (March 22, 1972). North American beikoku Shido-kan Karate-do Association. Retrieved August 24, 2008, from Biographies Web site: http://www.ihadojo.com/Origins/chibana.htm

Retrieved August 24, 2008, from Fiftiesweb Web site: http://www.fiftiesweb.com/pop/prices-1955.htm

Seishiro Okazaki. (2010, November 13). In Wikipedia, The Free Encyclopedia. Retrieved 01:51, May 26, 2011, from http://en.wikipedia.org/w/index.php?title=Seishiro_Okazaki&oldid=396500934

Shamisen. (2011, February 27). In Wikipedia, The Free Encyclopedia. Retrieved 02:42, March 16, 2011, from http://en.wikipedia.org/w/index.php?title=Shamisen&oldid=416162048

Yamaguchi Gogen. (2009, April 1). In Wikipedia, The Free Encyclopedia. Retrieved 01:52, May 26, 2011, from http://en.wikipedia.org/w/index.php?title=Yamaguchi_Gogen&oldid=281052664

www.ingramcontent.com/pod-product-compliance
Lightning Source LLC
Chambersburg PA
CBHW020202090426
42734CB00008B/912